Plasti(e)cological Thinking

Working out an (Infra)structural Geoerotics

Dr. Abhisek Ghosal

Christ (Deem to be University) (BGR Campus)
Bengaluru, India

Critical Perspectives on Social Science

VERNON PRESS

www.vernonpress.com

In the Americas:
Vernon Press
1000 N West Street, Suite 1200
Wilmington, Delaware, 19801
United States

In the rest of the world:
Vernon Press
C/Sancti Espiritu 17,
Malaga, 29006
Spain

Critical Perspectives on Social Science

Library of Congress Control Number: 2022950701

ISBN: 978-1-64889-719-1

Also available: 978-1-64889-596-8 [Hardback]; 978-1-64889-634-7 [PDF, E-Book]

Contents

Acknowledgements

I take this opportunity to express my heartfelt regards to those people who have helped me over the months in many ways with the preparation of this book, as I owe a lot to each of them. First of all, I would like to mention the constant support and inspiration of my father, Prof. Bhaskarjyoti Ghosal, a senior Professor at the Department of Sanskrit, the University of Burdwan, West Bengal, India. He has extended all kinds of help to me whenever I sought help from him. Moreover, he has played an instrumental role in guiding me to go through some Vedic and post-Vedic narratives–the readings of those seminal books belonging to the great traditions of Sanskrit literature helped me shaping up my thoughts and insights pertaining to the title of this book. He at once suggested I develop comparative models of enquiry so that densely mediated planetary ecology can better be comprehended and at times advised me to be cautious of the limits of theoretical formulations which sometimes take critical thinkers away from the praxis. I fondly remember that while I was revising the manuscript of the book and was rigorously brushing up some of my arguments, he advised me out of his long-standing experience in the field of research that 'brevity is the soul of wit' but oversimplification or excessive uses of theoretical jargons cannot but end up in redundancy. I have tried to keep these small but effective pieces of advice in mind while attempting to ground 'plasti(e)cological thinking' in ratiocination.

My mother, Arpita Ghosal, has been quite helpful all throughout my journey and catered good food and good thoughts to me whenever I felt a little bit tired of thinking and doing this book. Apart from her well-cooked dishes, she used to inspire me in every possible way so that I could immediately revive energy—both physical and psychological—to come back to my study stable.

I hereby duly acknowledge the roles of my esteemed teachers who have encouraged me in many ways both to pick up relevant thoughts and ideas from a plethora of books and to do away with clichéd and hackneyed insights wherever it was needed. For example, as far as Indic thoughts are concerned, Dr. Anway Mukhopadhayay's books —*The Authority of Female Speech in Indian Goddess Traditions: Devi and Womansplaining* and *The Goddess in Hindu-Tantric Traditions: Devi as Corpse*— helped me a lot in knowing different facets of Indic Traditions. Besides it, I feel indebted to Dr. Saswat Samay Das who has not just only introduced me to the theoretical world of Deleuze and Guattari but also has led me to mull over Deleuzo-Guattarian coinages afresh. Academic interactions with Dr. Das on several issues have been prolific and productive of new insights. He has actually taught me how to think critically and transversally across disciplines. I also drew help and encouragement from other professors like Prof. Narayan Chandra Nayek, Dr. Somdatta Bhattacharyya, Prof. Indrajit Dube, and so on.

I also humbly acknowledge that I have had academic interactions with some other professors, which is worth mentioning. For example, Dr. Arnab Kumar Sinha is one of my teachers who has been encouraging me right from my post-graduation days to take up out-of-the-box research topics very seriously. Apart from Dr. Arnab Kumar Sinha, some of the freely available online lectures of Prof. Ranjan Ghosh, Prof. Ian Buchanan, Prof. Claire Colebrook, Prof. Catherine Malabou, and Prof. Gayatri Chakravorty Spivak, helped me immensely in formulating several contentions that I have put forward in this book. I owe a lot to each of them.

My friends have been quite supportive to me and shared some valuable insights whenever I sought them. My thanks go to Ritam Sarkar, Chanchal De Boxi, Pratik Sarkar, Dipra Sarkhel, Arghya Bhattacharyya, Sudip Malik, and to name only a few, who helped me in keeping my mental composure intact over the months. Their valuable inputs facilitated me in rephrasing my contentions wherever it was needed.

I must also thank anonymous reviewers who have given me helpful suggestions and positive feedback. I acknowledge the tremendous efforts of all those who are associated with Vernon Press for taking up my book project thereby giving me a global platform to discuss and share my insights and thoughts concerning planetarity.

Introduction

Geopoetics is a field of inquiry that is increasingly inspiring new and in-
novative modes of practice and conceptualization . . . [it] launches a
multivocal investigation into the forms, theories, and poetics of earth-
making—because, at its etymological root, that is precisely what geopoetics is: Earth-making. (Magrane et al. 1)
Qualitative hyper-fractalization thus agglomerates the heterogeneous
qualifications in counterpoint to the topographical synaptic fractalization
producing new, artificial procedures of subjectification. (*Schizoanalytic
Cartographies*, Guattari 185)

Where does Ecopoetics stand today? How does it help one figure out ecological
complexities that find currency in post-neoliberal society? Does one still really
need to experiment in the field of planetarity soaked in ecopoetics? Does Ecopoetics still have much in store? Can "plasti(e)cological thinking" be taken into
account as a "portal" for making significant advancements in the field of (infra)structural geoerotics? These unsettling questions at once lead me to call the
futurity of stratified planetarity into question and at times direct me to engage
myself in the systematic deterritorialization and destratification of Ecopoetics.
This chapter seeks to offer a critical overview of the nascent state of Ecopoetics
in the ancient past and how it has been developing over time. In short, the ep-
igenetic progression of ecopoetical thoughts in the past is sharply pitted
against the contemporary epistemic strands of Ecopoetics that stand inflected
by critical theoretical "turns" so as to help readers understand continual epistemic folding and unfolding of "ecotheory" Different phases of development of
Ecopoetics are intended to be mapped to examine how Ecopoetics assumes a
number of critical dimensions in the process of differential becoming and consequently, how it stands wedded to the critico-epistemic frameworks of
geopoetics, thereby offering eco/geo-critical metamodels to respond to the
evolving eco/geo-logical crisis. Onto-epistemic becomings of Ecopoetics are
intended to be brought out to facilitate one to figure out why and how the contemporary figurations of Ecopoetics fail to offer effectual strategies to deal with
the insidious upshots of stratified planetary thinking. It is by destratifying and
deterritorializing contemporary ecopoetics, this manuscript aims at working
out an (infra)structural geoerotics that stands premised on the "zoegraphical"
insights in general and particularly on a micropoetics of bio-geo-eco-semiosis.
In a nutshell, this manuscript looks forward to rewiring "ecotheory" anew.

Ecopoetics Then

> What is "eco soma"? I approach this phrase as a mash-up, an encounter
> zone all by itself. . . . I propose "eco soma" as a method for working with
> somatics in performance. . . . In an eco soma enquiry . . . I am part of
> both a human and a non-human ecology and I am part of a set of his-
> torically and culturally grown relations. All of this brings embeddedness
> and entanglement. (Kuppers 1)

Whereas Kuppers seeks to comprehend "eco soma" in terms of human-non-
human "embeddedness" and "entanglement" thereby referring to the intensive "creative flights of connection" that "eco soma" embodies, one may be
reminded of the nascent stage of epistemic zones of "ecopoetics" which started
off in a sluggish fashion and most importantly, people of that time were not
quite conscious about of the critico-epistemic potentials of "ecopoetics" in examining ontico/ontological transhistoricality of the Earth. If one carefully
investigates the syntagmatic formation of the word "ecopoetics", he has to take
note of the two comprising words–ecology and poetics–both of which have
points of convergences and divergences but above all, "productive" conflation
between the two results in the configuration of a sort of epistemological framework which, generally, helps one make use of poetical insights to investigate
the continual becoming and unbecoming of the ecology through what Guattari
calls "enunciative fractalization" in *Schizoanalytic Cartographies*. Here, one
may argue that "ecopoetics" could be subsumed as the geo-aesthetic logic of
becoming that holds ecological entities up for the critical appreciation of readers. Following this contention, it needs to be stated that "ecopoetics" has been
understood by critical thinkers from various epistemological viewpoints. For
example, whereas in "Ecopoetics", Kate Rigby proposes to consider "ecopoetics" as "an ecocritical neologism" which calls for the incorporation of "an
ecological or environmental perspective" into "the study of poetics" (79), Timothy Morton moves up a step forward and contends in "Coexistence and
Coexistents: Ecology without a World": "Life forms are connected in a mesh
without a center or an edge. . . . Thinking ecology without worlds (singular and
plural) means thinking coexistence and intimacy in constant flux" (169). Morton's Heideggerian "eco-logic" in a way points at the chaosophical "plane of
immanence"–the veritable zone of operativity for "ecopoetics". Ecopoetics,
therefore, seems to offer a number of "zones of indiscernibility", allowing ecological and somatic elements to intersect each other at multiple points. It also
calls for the close study of poetic materials having eco-geo-logical underpinnings. It is true that Ecology has its distinctive sounds and colours, expressions

and receptions, and one needs to have "ecopoetical" sensibility to get to the bottom of all these. In "Introduction: The Language of Nature, the Nature of Language", Scott Knickerbocker reflectively argues:

> This rematerializing of language, one variety of defamiliarization, is of what many poets deliberately attempt: Poetry creates something of the conditions of hearing (not just listening to) a foreign language–we hear it as language, not music or noise; yet we cannot immediately process its meaning. Another way of saying this is that the poetic function–what Tsur calls 'the poetic mode of speech perception'–rematerializes language, returns it from 'speech' back to 'sound'. . . . (1-2)

This excerpt puts emphasis on the fact that Nature has its own language of expression which, far from being anthropocentric in nature, relates various conditions through Nature. . Keeping Knickerbocker's contention in mind, one may argue that the distinctive language of Nature has been prevalent since time immemorial but it has undergone substantial changes over the period of time.

One may trace varied figurations of "ecopoetical" sensibility in different ancient cultural and political scenarios when the term "Ecopoetics" did not come into being. For example, in the Vedic period, one of the richest and oldest human civilizations in the world, people were very much aware of the different components of Nature and were used to going by the laws of Nature. On the one hand, Vedic people could figure out subtle but palpable changes in Nature and on the other hand, they could finely work in tune with requirements of the Nature. They could, in a way, connect and reconnect themselves with Nature and most importantly, used to include Nature in religious, political, cultural, economic, and territorial activities. Vedic hymns in particular are reflective of the ecopoetical sensibility possessed by people of that time. For example, in *Ṛgveda*, it is depicted that "dawn", that is, ūṣā was used to be extolled in poetical terms. Descriptions of ūṣā in particular are reflective of how people used to observe the continual changes in the becoming(s) of ūṣā and used to admire its expansiveness across the world:

> What mortal, O immortal Dawn, enjoyeth thee? Where lovest thou?
> To whom, O radiant, dost thou go? (1.30.20, Griffith 18)
> For we have had thee in our thoughts whether anear or far away,
> Red-hued and like a dappled mare. (1.30.21, Griffith 18)

These Vedic hymns also suggest that the "dawn", being one of the important planetary events, used to work a lot of things, thereby directing and redirecting the lives of human and non-human entities alike. For example, the advent of "dawn" does not only dispel darkness thereby making the planet rise with the sun but also is essentially a timeless phenomenon and its radiance stands pervasive across the planet. In another hymn, ūṣā is held in high regard, for it is capable of guiding a herd of cows back in the fields; helping noble men riding chariots get fame; dispelling darkness; and driving animals and birds in different directions. It is because of the dawn's magnificent power, Kanvas call it with sacred songs:

> E'EN from above the sky's bright realm come, Usas, by auspicious ways:
> Let red steeds bear thee to the house of him who pours the Soma, juice.
> (1.49.1, Griffith 28)
> The chariot which thou mountest, fair of shape, O Usas light to move,-
> Therewith, O Daughter of the Sky, aid men of noble fame today. (1.49.2, Griffith 28)
> Bright Usas, when thy times return, all quadrupeds and bipeds stir,
> And round about flock winged birds from all the boundaries of heaven.
> (1.49.3, Griffith 29)
> Thou dawning with thy beams of light illumest all the radiant realm.
> Thee, as thou art, the Kanvas, fain for wealth, have called with sacred songs. (1.49.4, Griffith 29)

So, it is clear that Vedic people used to take ūṣā into account, for ūṣā, apart from being a planetary phenomenon, has been deeply associated with the anthropocentric understanding of the planet. Interestingly, Vedic people used to eulogize ūṣā in particular because the advent of ūṣā used to spread positive energy among human and non-human entities.

Ecological consciousness of Vedic people gets reflected in their worshipping of Agni, that is, the fire which virtually regulates all sorts of human activities. Interestingly, ecological approaches to the enormity of Agni are couched in poetical terms:

> Through Agni man obtaineth wealth, yea, plenty waxing day by day,
> Most rich in heroes, glorious. (1.1.3, Griffith 3)
> Ruler of sacrifices, guard of Law eternal, radiant One,
> Increasing in thine own abode. (1.1.4, Griffith 3)
> Be to us easy of approach, even as a father to his son:
> Agni, be with us for our weal. (1.4.5, Griffith 3)

Different roles of Agni have duly been acknowledged in an ecopoetical fashion in that these hymns were meant to deify Agni. It was believed that Agni, being the radiant One, used to play important roles in helping people conduct rituals of all sorts. What is interesting is that Vedic people were very much engaged in understanding ecological components of the planet in poetic terms. In addition to it, Vāyu, that is, air, was used to be regarded with high esteem because the flow of air, as it was understood by Vedic sages, has been immensely important for doing ritualistic activities, apart from maintaining planetary equilibrium:

> Knowing the days, with Soma juice poured forth, the singers glorify
> Thee, Vayu, with their hymns of praise. (1.2.1, Griffith 3)

The god of sky, thunder, war, and storm, among others, that is, Indra, too, was hugely worshipped in Vedic times possibly because Vedic sages could comprehend the might of Indra in safeguarding living and non-living entities on the planet. In one of the important Vedic hymns, Indra was declared to have no enemy and was the god who has been continuously increasing its own strength:

> I SING thy fame that, Maghavan, through thy Greatness the heavens and
> earth invoked thee in their terror,
> Thou, aiding Gods, didst quell the power of Dasas, what time thou
> helpest many a race, O Indra. (10.54.1, Griffith 448)
> When thou wast roaming, waxen strong in body, telling thy might, Indra,
> among the people,
> All that men called thy battles was illusion: no foe hast thou to-day, nor
> erst hast found one (10.54.2, Griffith 448)

These hymns vouch for the overarching presence of Indra who has been looking after the Earth either by giving positive strength to the priests who used to take part in rituals or by taking strength away from the Dasa race. Varuṇa, the god of ocean, justice and truth, was used to be taken into cognizance, for, along with Indra, Varuṇa has been in the charge of rain required for the sustenance of life on the Earth:

> Mitra, of holy strength, I call, and foe-destroying Varuna,
> Who make the oil-fed rite complete. (1.2.7, Griffith 3)

It is therefore clear that Vedic people were quite conscious of the interconnected roles of Agni, Vāyu, Indra and Varuṇa—subtle interplay among the celestial figures has been instrumental in pulling the planet up from being caught in an entropy.

In fact, Vedic people had the required ecopoetical sensibility for figuring out the cosmology of the Earth. Apart from understanding the planet in terms of "dvyāpṛithibi,"[1] they engaged themselves in deciphering the eternal Truth that holds the world to the laws of Nature:

> THE Father of the eye, the Wise in spirit, created both these worlds submerged in fatness.
> Then when the eastern ends were firmly fastened, the heavens and the earth were far extended. (10.82.1, Griffith 462)
> May this my truthful speech guard me on every side wherever heaven and earth and days are spread abroad.
> All else that is in motion finds a place of rest: the waters ever flow and ever mounts the Sun. (10.37.2, Griffith 439)

These Vedic hymns reflect how the ecological and cosmological events were understood in terms of poetic sensibility and how these ecopoetical understandings were intricately tied to the questions of survival and sustenance. Vedic ecopoetical consciousness was also extended to the discrete topographical features of the planet and thus particular references to different rivers and their benefits to the Vedic civilization can be traced in *Ṛgveda*:

> All sacrificial viands wait on Agni as the Seven mighty Rivers seek the ocean.
> Not by our brethren was our food discovered: find with the Gods care for us, thou who knowest. (1.71.7, Griffith 39)
> O Soma, these Seven Rivers flow, as being thine, to give command:
> The Streams of milk run forth to thee. (9.66.6, Griffith 392)
> Coming together, glorious, loudly roaring - Sarasvati, Mother of Floods, the seventh
> With copious milk, with fair streams, strongly flowing, full swelling with the volume of their water (7.36.6, Griffith 270)

These Vedic hymns clearly suggest the multifaceted roles of the seven rivers in retaining the existence of "life" on the planet. Poetic descriptions of the flows of different rivers remind one of how Vedic sages used to integrate ecological consciousness with the topographical specificities of the planet Earth. Interestingly, these hymns also indicate that Vedic sages used to try to figure out the language of the planet Earth, and distinctive manifestations of the planet Earth through the processual developments of different planetary entities and were quite acquainted with eco-aesthetic dimensions of planet Earth. Ecopoetical sensibility of Vedic people was inclusive of the aesthetic appreciation of the movements of the sun which does not only cater light and warmth to the dwellers of the planet but also enhances the in-built beauties of the planet as well:

> The one departeth and the other cometh: unlike in hue day's, halves march on successive.
> One hides the gloom of the surrounding Parents. Dawn on her shining chariot is resplendent. (1.123.7, Griffith 68)
> The same in form to-day, the same tomorrow, they still keep Varuna's eternal statute. Blameless, in turn they traverse thirty regions, and dart across the spirit in a moment. (1.123.8, Griffith 68)
> She who hath knowledge of the first day's nature is born refulgent white from out the darkness.
> The Maiden breaketh not the law of Order, day by day coming to the place appointed. (1.123.9, Griffith 68)
> In pride of beauty like a maid thou goest, O Goddess, to the God who longs to win thee,
> And smiling youthful, as thou shinest brightly, before him thou discoverest thy bosom. (1.123.10, Griffith 68)

These Vedic hymns reflect Vedic sages used to fall back on their ecopoetical understanding of the planet Earth while trying to come to terms with different planetary phenomena.

Since Vedic period, ecopoetics has been gradually taking shape and getting inflected by the advent of new epistemological schools of thought. Consequently, the figuration and configuration of Ecopoetics started to alter and became inclusive of literary studies. Kālidāsa, one of the greatest Sanskrit poets, penned down some remarkable works like *Meghdūtaṃ, Ṛtusamhāram, Abhijñāmśakuntalaṃ,* and so on, which reflect his deep ecological awareness. Ecopoetics which began to get unfolded in Vedic times got reshaped by Kālidāsa who exhibits ecopoetical sensibility at the outset of *Ṛtusamhāram*:

> The sun is blazing fiercely,
> the moon longed for eagerly,
> deep waters inviting
> to plunge in continually,
> days drawing to a close in quiet beauty
> the tide of desire running low:
> scorching Summer is now here, my love.

. . .
Hearts burning in the fire of separation,
men far from home can scarcely bear to see
the swirling clouds of dust tossed up
from the earth burnt by the sun's fierce heat. (Rajan 105-106)

Opening lines of *Ṛtusamhāram* lay bare ecopoetical weaving of the personal
desires with the planetary events thereby making attempts to connect with the
world around. Ecopoetical references to the sun, the moon and waters remind
one of how all these were used to be taken into account with high regards by
Vedic sages and subsequently suggest that the development of the speaker's
personal emotions stands in conformity with the transformations of the Earth
in general. In *Ṛtusamhāram*, one may find that the close observations of the
speaker on the passage of time followed by the movements of "Summer",
"Rains", "Autumn", "Winter" and "Spring" are captured in connection with the
maturing of the desire of the lover for the beloved. One may also be reminded
of another passage from *Meghdūtaṃ* which, too, lays down an ecopoetical de-
piction of the cloud which performs like a messenger:

4
With the month of rains approaching
desiring to sustain his beloved's life,
hoping to send glad tidings of his wellbeing
through the life-giving cloud, he made with reverence
an offering of fresh blossoms of wild jasmine,
prefacing it with words of affection
and joyously welcomed the cloud.
5
Blended of mists and light, winds and water
can a mere cloud bear messages
that only the living with keen senses
and intelligence can convey?
Unmindful of this the yaksa entreated it,
overwhelmed by unreasoning eagerness;
indeed, the love-sick, their minds clouded,
confuse the sentient with the insentient. (Rajan 137-138)

These quoted excerpts attest to the fact that the speaker chooses the cloud as a
messenger for sending love to his beloved. More importantly, the act of choos-
ing a planetary component like a cloud for delivering love to the distant

beloved is suggestive of inseparable connectivity between human desire and planetary acts in the sense that the "living-giving" potentials of the cloud are instrumentalized to make it carry human desires to a distant beloved. The transport(ability) of the cloud was utilized by Yaksa who was able to infuse "human affection" into the actions of the cloud, the "Rain-Giver".

Having analyzed the development of Ecopoetics along the development of Sanskrit literature, it is found that although the term Ecopoetics comes into being late in academia, some of the strands of Ecopoetics have been in existence since Vedic times. One may also find that Ecopoetical thoughts gradually develop either by assuming new epistemological dimensions or discarding some hackneyed dimensions. For example, whereas in Vedic times, ritualistic celebrations of ecopoetical thoughts were used to be carried out, the writings of Kālidāsa suggest the preponderances of affect, intellect and percept in the figurations of Ecopoetical thoughts. What is interesting here to note is that the advancement of Ecopoetical sensibility was steeped in anthropocentric mapping of the planet Earth and was not in conflict with the ideological strands of Anthropocentrism. Sanskritic traditions also inform us that early ecopoetical insights are reflective of an ecological consciousness which incorporates the co-existence of all human and non-human planetary entities. Apart from it, ancient figurations of ecopoetical thoughts embedded in Sanskritic literary traditions are divested of interdisciplinarity in terms of thinking and were broadly celebrations of human-ecology continuum. In a nutshell, it was very much limited to the poetic recognition of the mutual exclusivity existing between human beings and planetary ecology and subsequently to the imposition of human "emotions" onto the individualities of different natural entities like the sun, the cloud, rivers, and so on.

Ecopoetics Now

Ecology without Nature . . . helps us to see that "nature" is an arbitrary rhetorical construct, empty of independent, genuine existence behind or beyond the texts we create about it. The rhetoric of nature depends upon something I define as an *ambient poetics*, a way of conjuring up a sense of a surrounding atmosphere or world. (Morton 21-22)

The Earth is undergoing a period of intense techno-scientific transformations. If no remedy is found, the ecological disequilibrium this has generated will ultimately threaten the continuation of life on the planet's surface. (*The Three Ecologies*, Guattari 27)

The 'posthuman turn'–defined as the convergence of posthumanism with postanthropocentrism–is a complex and multidirectional

discursive and material event. It encourages us to build on the generative potential of the critiques of humanism developed by radical
epistemologies that aim at a more inclusive practice of becoming-human. (Bignall and Braidotti 1)

Ecopoetics in contemporary times can simply be understood as an epistemic
conflation of both ecology[2] and poetics, which lays down critical frameworks
for delving deep into the representation of ecology through poetical means.
Ecopoetical insights generally help one understand how fluid configurations of
ecology find "literary" manifestations in different epistemological traditions.
With the advent of economic globalization followed by the rapid growth of human migration owing to technological advancements and relaxation of
security at national borders, ecological concerns started to gain currency in the
academic parlances. A group of ecological thinkers, being moved by certain
apocalyptic assumptions, began to take up ecological issues seriously and
made significant advancements in the sphere of "ecotheory". An understanding of Ecopoetics therefore cannot be complete without taking recourse to
contemporary historical developments of "ecocriticism". One cannot but be
reminded of Cheryll Glotfelty who, along with other ecocritical thinkers, attempts to figure out contemporaneous inflections on ecopoetics. She reflects
in "Introduction: Literary Studies in an Age of Environmental Crisis" that: ". . .
ecocriticism is the study of the relationship between literature and the physical
environment" (xviii). Glotfelty's definition can be interpreted in two ways: she
is very much interested in putting the critical spotlight on the "relationship"
between literature and physical environment; she subtly clubs together literature and its physical surroundings in a dialectical format as it were in the sense
that literature stands in contrast with its physical surroundings which occa-
sionally inform and impact the making of different literary works. It may also
be possible that she deliberately strikes up a dialectical connection between
literature and its physical surroundings in order to pull "ecology" back from
being a *hackneyed metaphor*. She has tried to justify her preference for "eco"
over "environ", thereby implying that she very much looks forward to bringing
up "ecological" insights to redefine "human" perception of "Nature":

Furthermore, in its connotations, environ- is anthropocentric and du-
alistic, implying that we humans are at the center, surrounded by
everything that is not us, the environment. Eco-, in contrast, implies
interdependent communities, integrated systems, and strong connections among constituent parts. (xx)

It suggests that Glotfelty's choice of the word "eco" is contingent upon her preference for *interdependence, integration* and *connectivity* existing in the "relationship" between literature and its physical surroundings. She also reflects on "ecotheory" in this article to suggest that consideration of ecotheoretical constructs might help ecocritics to forge a path of its own. Although Glotfelty sets the tone for the emergence of Ecocriticism as a distinct critical school, her interventions in the formulation of some ecocritical notions are fraught with flaws, in my view. For example, she has forged a binary relationship between Nature and Culture, intending to foreground how domineering patterns of human culture have subsided Nature over time. What is interesting is that Glotfelty puts emphasis on Nature because she thinks that the Nature-centric approach might help human beings to explore the nuances in the relationship between literature and its physical environment. Following the trail of Glotfelty, William Rueckert, too, holds in "Literature and Ecology: An Experiment in Ecocriticism": "The problem now, as most ecologists agree, is to find ways of keeping the human community from destroying the natural community, and with it the human community" (107). Unlike Glotfelty, Rueckert reflects on "literary ecology" which stands striated with the rhizomatic flows of energy. He happens to be one of the early ecocritics who talks about the crux of ecopoetics in the following terms:

> A poem is stored energy, a formal turbulence, a living thing, a swirl in the flow. Poems are part of the energy pathways which sustain life. Poems are a verbal equivalent of fossil fuel (stored energy), but they are a renewable source of energy, coming, as they do, from those ever generative twin matrices, language and imagination. (108)

Rueckert's ecopoetical concerns are worth noting because he could initially think of having ecopoetics by working out "energy thinking" in a systematic fashion. His notion of "literary ecology" is further taken up by ecocritics from different perspectives.

While responding to the question "Is Nature Necessary?", Dana Philips reflectively argues: "But thinking and working our way through the past, and the perhaps unthinkable, impossible future of nature, may be our last best hope for building dwelling thinking here and now" (222). Philips is of this standpoint that in the time of imminent Environmental crisis, the importance of "nature" can hardly be relegated to insignificance. "Dwelling thinking" seems to be effective in dealing with environmental challenges, for it stands in tune with the requirements of "literary ecology". "Dwelling thinking" is also connotative of the intervention of topographical and spatial aspects into the construction of "literary ecology". "Literary ecology" is an *intellectual* plenum which gives room to different kinds of ecopoetical experimentations. Writing and re-writing "literary ecology" could be a roadmap for holding "Nature" back from ecological crisis. Rightly has Scott Russell Sanders argued in "Speaking a Word for Nature":

> It may seem quaint, in the age of megalopolis, to write about wilderness or about life on farms and in small towns; and it may seem escapist to write about distant planets where the environment shapes every human gesture; but such writing seems to me the most engaged and forward-looking we have. (195)

Sanders's viewpoint seems to me reasonable on the ground that a literary space is required for mapping out various strands of ecopoetics and interestingly, "literary ecology" caters a ground to ecocritics to reflect on ecology.

It is true that the development of Ecopoetics got institutionalized only after the advancement of Ecocritical movements across the world. In "Introduction: Literary Studies in an Age of Environmental Crisis", Glotfelty perceptively attempts to connect ecocritical thinking with the existing perceptions of Ecopoetical thoughts thereby opening up the horizon of "Ecotheory":

> Yet another theoretical project attempts to develop an ecological poetics, taking the science of ecology, with its concept of the ecosystem and its emphasis on interconnections and energy flow, as a metaphor for the way poetry functions in society. Ecocritics are also considering the philosophy currently known as deep ecology, exploring the implications that its radical critique of anthropocentrism might have for literary study. (xxiv)

This critical reflection indicates that ecological thinking in particular has been instrumental in framing the epistemological contour of Ecopoetics which gets turned out as a domain of interdisciplinary research, inviting scholars working on "science of ecology" or "ecosystem" or "energy flow" to make significant contributions. Unlike Sanskritic literary traditions, Ecopoetics which began to develop after the 1990s as a distinctive method of critical enquiry started to deviate from its erstwhile figurations and configurations and was inclined to incorporate critical thinking paradigms so as to delve deeper into the planetary phenomena. For example, in an engaging article titled "Beyond Ecology: SELF, PLACE, AND THE PATHETIC FALLACY", Neil Evernden reflects: "The subversive nature of Ecology rests on its assumption of literal interrelatedness, not just interdependence. Ecology as a discipline has been called upon to ignore the former and deal with the latter, on the assumption that the patterns of dependence can be shifted, whereas relatedness cannot" (102-103). This critical reflection clearly suggests that ecocritical thinking has to revolve round and celebrate "interrelatedness" instead of "interdependence" simply because the "patterns of dependence" could be produced and reproduced culturally and politically, thereby incurring the possibility of homogenization. Put it in other words, it is the "interrelatedness" which multiplies the possibility of heterogeneous production and reproduction of ecological insights. Besides it, this sense of "interrelatedness" is charged with "lines of flight" and therefore can hardly be territorialized. Evernden's critical contention could be linked up to the case of Ecopoetics which also insists that there lies a sort of "interrelatedness" between ecological thinking and poetic sensibility and eventually, it happens to be the operative logic of Ecopoetics. Moreover, "interrelatedness" seems to be productive of new combinations of ecopoetical thoughts which can be of profound import in reconfiguring human understanding the planet Earth.

The domain of Ecopoetics, later on, got extended to the domains of discursive formation in that with the advancements of Poststructuralism, scholars became engaged in enframing "ecology" with the help of certain political codings and consequently, became interested in de-rooting ecology from the Nature and subsequently in re-rooting them in political discourses. Kate Soper happens to be one important thinker who contends in "Representing Nature": ". . . the deconstruction of misleading cultural representations of 'nature' is also implicitly recommending an alternative and improved cognition – a mode of understanding that will acknowledge the discursive construction of 'nature'. . ." (62). Soper is actually critical of the discursive understanding of "Nature" simply because it cannot fully address the "ecological crisis" induced by the pervasive trajectories of capitalism, industrialization and urbanization. Within the paradigm of ecological thinking, Soper shrewdly brings in ecopolitical questions to interrogate discursive mapping of the "interrelatedness" existing among human and non-human beings on the planet. Greg Garrard moves up a step forward and posits the ecopolitical question of authentic representation of "Nature" in the context of emergent postmodern ecology which:

> . . . neither returns us to the ancient myth of the Earth Mother . . . nor supplies us with evidence that "nature knows best" . . . [this irony] only increases the scope and extent of our liability as the most powerful species on the planet. The poetics of authenticity assumes . . . that there is a fixed external standard we ought to try and meet. The poetics of

responsibility recognises that every inflection of Earth is our inflection,
every standard our standard. . . . (178-179).

This contention leads one to think of the way the act of representation inscribes
critical dimensions of Ecopoetics which puts emphasis on striking a balance
between "the poetics of authenticity" and "the poetics of responsibility". Contemporary figurations of Ecopoetics imply that ecopoetical sensibility does not
stand confined in the domain of aesthetics but tends to figure in ecopolitical,
ecotheoretical and ecoterritorial concerns in it. The advent of technology in
particular, impacts the epistemological transformation of Ecopoetics which is
coerced to comply with the technological framework which ". . . is inherently
expansionist and can reveal only by reduction. Its aim is to enclose all beings
in a particular availability and manipulability" (Conley 67).

   This act of "enframing" results in the territorialization of Ecopoetics to an extent in that Ecopoetics is provincially reduced to the domains of "availability"
and "manipulability". Unlike Conley, Garrard rightly brings in Heideggerian
ecophilosophy to enrich ecocritical thinking–". . . [there lies] the fundamental
difference between mere material existence and a revelation of 'being' or the
thing-ness of things" (31)–an important strand which could be taken into account to comprehend how Ecopoetics tends to address the sharp tension
between onticological and ontological dimensions embodied by different
planetary entities. In short, Ecopoetics helps one engage himself/herself in going beyond the bounds of either onticological or ontological tenets of any
planetary body. It also implies that Ecopoetics in actuality encourages scholars
to evade the snares of codification and to engage with the "interrelatedness"
among planetary bodies.[3]

   Interestingly, the jurisdiction of Ecopoetics does not stand limited to mere
aesthetic appreciation of planetary bodies but pushes one to critically engage
with the fluid intersections among planetary bodies and events. For example,
in "The Angel and the Storm: 'Material Spirit' in the Era of Climate Change",
Tom Cohen correctly remarks that ecology is connected with economics so
much so that any disruption in economic activity is bound to leave a dreadful
impact on ecological becoming(s) of different planetary bodies. What Cohen
actually does is that the domain of ecology is deliberately delimited to the
sphere of economics which cuts across the developments of the planet Earth:
". . . [the] interplay between the economic and ecological, the 'eco-eco' disas-
ter, tends to occlude the exponential curves of issues that lie outside the
screen–collapsing marine life, mass extinction events, 'peak' everything (oil,
humans, water . . .), projections of 'population culling,' and so on" (129). The

concerns of Cohen could be explained in this way that ecocatastrophes require ecopoetical attention not just only because these are upshots of a number of densely interconnected ecological factors but also because these provoke scholars and critical thinkers to mull over possible ways of dealing with eco-catastrophes ecopoetically. Ranjan Ghosh is one important thinker who has attempted to connect the idea of "new nature" with "poetic creativity" in "Globing the Earth: The New Eco-logics of Nature", thereby laying down an open space for Ecopoetics to operate:

> Sequestering nature from human intervention is clearly impossible, hence the need to create a "new nature": a dynamic, functional nature, revised and devised–supported by human technology and made sustainable in the face of human growth and commercial exploitation. This lends a certain tension to the cataclysmic prospect of the "unborn" (phobic) incarnation of nature and the nature that is being "helped" in its birthing; this is an ecotechnical genesis–the one in the process of being born conflated with the "yet to be born." (5)

Ghosh's contention calls for an "ecotechnical genesis" which speaks of the coming together of "being born" and "yet to be born". In other words, Ghosh subtly suggests that Ecopoetics stands in quest of "new eco-logics" in the inter-relatedness among different planetary bodies. Taking Ghosh's contention into account, it can be argued that strands of Ecopoetics are nowadays in dialogue with technological innovations carried out by human beings and thus seem to be capable of catering to new critical frameworks for probing the impacts of advanced technology on the health of the planet.

In "Un-natural Ecopoetics Natural/Cultural Intersections in Poetic Language and Form", Sarah Nolan proposes the concept of "un-natural ecopoetics" which ". . . investigates how poets attempt to use unique forms to capture the multiplicity and complexity of lived experience as closely as possible while simultaneously foregrounding the textual space in which such expression occurs" (88). Unlike traditional ecopoetical expressions, "un-natural ecopoetics" allows ecopoets to focus ". . . on various situations in which individual memory, personal experience, ideology, and the limitations of the senses intermingle with natural elements of experience and on how new forms and experimentation with language can work to express these facets of experience as accurately as possible" (88). So, it is clear that this emergent figuration of Ecopoetics concentrates on the intermingling of "individual memory" and "personal experience" with "natural elements of experience" thereby trying to forge "new forms" of expression that the Earth puts to uses. At this point, one may be reminded of that contemporary figurations of Ecopoetics stand inflected by New Materialism and thus, it celebrates "... the mutuality of texts and contexts, or in the way environments are crisscrossed by poetic language" (88). Nolan exclusively points at how Ecopoetics today seeks to embrace ideological strands of New Materialism conditioned by the overwhelming presences of technology, economic globalization, and "cultural shifts":

> In order to account for new environments brought on by technology, globalization, politics, and cultural shifts, ecopoetics must broaden its understanding of "environment" ... embracing the new materialisms that integrate the human into the complicated and multidirectional networks of experience. (89)

This excerpt makes it clear that the domain of Ecopoetics nowadays gets extended to New Materialist understanding of the mediatedness of "the complicated and multidirectional networks of experience". The expansiveness of Ecopoetics can once again be elaborated taking recourse to "Introduction New International Voices in Ecocriticism" where Serpil Oppermann, while working out ecocritical consciousness in the present time, contends: "In this context, the particular theories in circulation today–neo-bioregionalism, eco-cosmopolitanism, eco-mimesis, postcolonial ecocritique, prismatic ecology, and material ecocriticism–are hybrid forms with different but also interrelated ecocritical approaches" (8). This is quite true in the context of Ecopoetics which has so much to offer to scholars by being integrated with critical thinking paradigms like eco-cosmopolitanism, material ecocriticism, and prismatic ecology, among others. Here, one may be reminded of J. Scott Bryson's *The West Side of Any Mountain: Place, Space, and Ecopoetry* which offers the most comprehensive understanding of Ecopoetics today in the following words:

> Ecopoetry is a mode that, while adhering to certain conventions of traditional nature poetry, advances beyond that tradition and takes on distinctly contemporary problems and issues, thus becoming generally marked by three primary characteristics: an ecological and biocentric perspective recognizing the interdependent nature of the world; a deep humility with regard to our relationships with human and non-human nature; and an intense scepticism toward hyperrationality, a scepticism that usually leads to condemnation of an over technologized modern world and a warning concerning the very real potential for ecological catastrophe. (2)

Bryson's critical engagement with specificities of Ecopoetics can be corroborated by arguing that Ecopoetics can at once be taken into account as a critical lens required for looking into the becoming(s) of the Earth and can at times be held as a way of "being with" the nuanced intersections between human and non-human bodies.[4]

Deterritorializing Ecopoetics

Ecopoetics stands on the edge in the global academia, for existing models of ecopoetics cannot help one address emerging problems in the post-neoliberal society. For instance, existing models of ecopoetics can only help one understand how human beings tend to *represent* ecological entities in the terrain of "literary ecology". In other words, ecopoetical frameworks within "literary ecology" cannot help one figure out how non-human beings of ecology play instrumental roles in governing "geokinetic" movements of the Earth. The "intensive becoming" of ecological agents cannot be figured in terms of existing ecopoetical models of inquiry. Sometimes, different anthropogenic wastes including plastics wreck havoc on the *differential intensity* of ecology. Prevailing frameworks of Ecopoetics only provide insights conducive to figuring out how human beings have literarily constructed "Nature" in different literary works. Kate Soper thus argues in "Representing Nature" that ecocritics can provide representational construction of Nature as "otherness" (61). Apart from it, the "Posthuman turn" in Literary Studies has made the function of Ecopoetics all the more difficult in the sense that it nowadays cannot aptly refer to how non-human agencies seek to rise to the occasion. In other words, ecopoetical insights do not seem to me adequate enough for taking stock of cultural, political and economic turns in the Humanities. Ecopoetics also stands divested of eco-geo-philosophical perspectives that are of profound import for comprehending how the networked operations of non-human beings render ecology at stake. In short, ecopoetics cannot offer ways through which the territory of "literary ecology" could be stretched off to some extent. New challenges of post-neoliberalism like the spreading of an energopolitical framework across the world and liberalization of the national economy, among others, can hardly be addressed through ecopoetical means. Following this critical contention, one may be reminded of the enormous potentials of Ecopoetics that have not got fully exhausted and thus these can be made operational even in recent times by means of experimentations which are supposed to open up new critical vistas for ecocritics. Besides it, theoretical experimentations within Ecopoetics can help it survive through new and upcoming challenges. More importantly, the inoperativity of Ecopoetics in the current times necessitates theoretical experimentation with Ecopoetics. This actually lays the foundation for "plasti(e)cological thinking" to turn up in the ecological discourses. In order to make room for "plasti(e)cological thinking" to operate within the politico-cultural and social discourses, "literary ecology" has to be systematically and categorically deterritorialized. The act of deterritorializing "literary ecology" cannot be done without taking note of Timothy Morton's persuasive argument in *Ecology Without Nature: Rethinking Environmental Aesthetics*: "*Ecology without Nature* argues that the very idea of 'nature' which so many hold dear will have to wither away in an 'ecological' state of human society" (1). Unlike Dana Philips, Morton holds that Nature has to take leave letting ecology run into politico-cultural and social affairs. It is the very "otherized" and constructed dimensions of Nature, which does not let ecology get deterritorialized along the "plane of Immanence". Deterritorialization of Ecopoetics in particular is needed to question how human beings have coded and overcoded the ecology *out there* and to shatter the dialectical interplay between literature and ecology. Here, one may be asked some perturbing questions: *does literature stand outside ecology or does ecology exclude literature? Does literature in actuality stand in a post-dialectical and post-natural relationship with ecology?* These questions are intended to be used as epistemic interstices for deterritorializing Ecopoetics to an extent so that "plasti(e)cological thinking" can finely fit into it. Theoretical contextualization of "plasti(e)cological thinking" is also intended to be laid out in such a way so that scholars may find it as a "portal" to the imminent world.

Deterritorializing Ecopoetics entails categorical erasure of strata and codes by means of which Ecopoetics is held different from other variants of Ecocriticism. In *Three Ecologies*, Guattari explains the notion of "ecosophy"– ". . . the environment, social relations and human subjectivity. . ." (28)–the intersecting trajectories among these need to be taken into account to comprehend the tension between "continuous development of new technoscientific means . . . on the surface of the planet" and "the inability of organized social forces and constituted subjective formations to take hold of these resources" (31). Guattarian observation on "ecosophy" can be integrated into the act of deterritorializing Ecopoetics because it helps one delimit Ecopoetics to some extent so as to meet "the demands of singularities" (31). In "Introduction Transnational Ecopoetics", Isabel Sobral Campos has ingeniously attempted to posit Ecopoetics in the transnational contexts, thereby hinting at the necessity for deterritorializing Ecopoetics to broaden its scope and operation across the Earth: She argues that Ecopoetics needs to be decentered so as to examine "ecologically informed modes of relating to the world" and the ". . . interactions between the human and non-human as well as mind and matter" (x). This contention could be consolidated by reminding one of Bernd Herzogenrath's understanding of "white ecology" which:

> . . . might provide a context in which different ecologies (different eco-
> logical fields, such as human, viral, chemical, etc., that all follow their
> own logics and trajectories) resonate with each other. An ecology moti-
> vated by the philosophy of Gilles Deleuze and Felix Guattari, I argue,
> can provide such a space–it is basically a call to think complexity, and
> to complex thinking, a way to think the environment as a negotiation of
> dynamic arrangements of cultural and natural forces, of both non-hu-
> man and human stressors and tensors, both of which are informed and
> "intelligent". (1)

Herzogenrath's critical formulation, that is, "white ecology" can well be used to deterritorialize the domain of Ecopoetics in that the integration of "white ecology" with the operation of Ecopoetics makes the latter incorporate the nuanced interactions among a variety of ecologies under its jurisdiction. In other words, Ecopoetics has to recognize dynamicity and fluidity embodied in earthly matters, for ". . . the matter is not inert in the first place but informed, for it consistently contains and produces emergent structures and potentials . . ." (6). Herzogenrath also comments on the intersections between white ecology and Ecopoetics in the following words: ". . . a 'white' mode of ecology, focusing on the autopoietic potential of matter . . . can account for the world's order and creativity without taking recourse to essentialism or determinism, nor to any transcendentalisms, since 'life' for Deleuze is the very property of matter itself" (6). Following this observation, it can be tenably put forward that instead of exclusively focusing on the particularities of the environment, the deterritorialization of Ecopoetics has to entail a close examination of the pervasive, invasive and diffusive nature of "life" through planetary "matters". This argument can be validated by drawing references to "zoegraphy" which, it is claimed by Louis Van Den Hengel in "Zoegraphy: Per/forming Posthuman Lives", is a:

> . . . a mode of writing life that is not indexed on the traditional notion of
> *bios*–the discursive, social, and political life appropriate to human be-
> ings–but which centers on the generative vitality of *zoe*, an inhuman,
> impersonal, and inorganic force which . . . is not specific to human life-
> worlds, but cuts across humans animals, technologies, and things.
> *Zoegraphy* is my attempt to confront the question of how to think and
> how to write a life that does not have any human body or self at its

center, a life which is in fact fundamentally inhuman, yet which connects human life to the immanent forces of a vital materiality. (2)

Keeping this viewpoint in mind, it is argued that Ecopoetics has to give in "zoegraphical" inroads into the transformations of planetary matters. The
configuration of contemporary Ecopoetics has to be constructed in such a way
that it can relate to the complex assemblages embedded in the Earth.

Deterritorializing Ecopoetics entails an epistemic refashioning of planetarity
which nowadays finds steep currency in conformity with the rise of post-anthropocentric thoughts. Rightly has Dipesh Chakrabarty observed in *The
Climate of History in a Planetary Age* that it is the need of the hour to critically
engage oneself with ". . . an awareness of the planet and of its geobiological
history" (1) spanned across varied temporalities and to investigate the devel-
opmental geo-histories of the humanity at large.[5] Among other species found
on the planet Earth, human beings stand superior to the rest and seek to order
and reorder, form and transform, embody and disembody, territorialize and
deterritorialize the planet Earth in order to sustain their territorial govern
(mentality) in every form intact, and moreover, their continual attempts to in-
vade into the intensive becoming(s) of the planet result in bio-geo-eco-logical
catastrophes. The predominance of human beings on the planet, with the help
of techno-commercial connectivity, in short, questions the prevailing anthropocentric worldviews and subsequently, pushes humanity to mull over the
material/discursive interconnectedness among human, transhuman, posthuman, non-human, and ahuman entities. Planetary illness, in particular, has
been a cause of concern for humanity not just only because it demands a series
of entwined ethicopolitical frameworks required to cultivate ethical and legiti-
mate ways of knowing the Earth but also because it pushes concerned human
beings to weigh the possibility of multispecies worlding as a means for exploring the crux of planarity. It is intended to be explored in this work that the
epistemic integration of Ecopoetics with the strands of planetarity is supposed
to result in the opening up of the field of Ecopoetics to the concerns of planetary thinking which primarily deals with the nuanced becoming(s) of the planet
induced by the exploitative and vicious activities of human beings among others.

Deterritorialized Ecopoetical framework can, in many ways, help one recon-
figure planetary thinking so as to withstand the strikes of dire and dreadful
ecological catastrophes. For example, Ecopoetics is capable of offering a sort of
micropoetics–an understanding of which proves instrumental in spelling out
the "immanent micropolitics" embodied in the ceaseless transformation of the

planet through time and space. Moreover, the deterritorialization of Ecopoetics is supposed to turn planetary thinking into a veritable "war machine" which would make room for "plasti(e)cological thinking" to operate amidst planetary concerns. In this regard, it needs to be mentioned that "plasti(e)cological thinking", being held as a matter of lived experience and as an epistemic framework, seems to be able to upgrade and update planetary thinking thereby making a significant contribution to the domain of New Earth Politics. "Plasti(e)cological thinking", it is claimed, has the distinctive potential to ground Ecopoetics in praxis, for it stands invasive, diffusive, and pervasive among the entwined and diverse ecologies on the Earth.[6]

This present study is designed to be split up into different chapters which dwell on different aspects relating to the grounding of Ecopoetics through the mediation of "plasti(e)cological thinking" for enhancing the efficacy of planetary thinking. In the Introduction, genealogical progress of ecopoetical consciousness is mapped out, negotiating a variety of literary and cultural traditions. Epistemological mapping of Ecopoetics is followed by the deterritorialization of the same in order to make room for "plasti(e)cological thinking" to come into being. In short, epistemological limitations of Ecopoetics are pointed out so as to lay the ground for the theorization of "plasti(e)cological thinking" thereby working out an (infra)structural geoerotics. In the first chapter titled "Theoretical 'Turns' to Stratified Planetary Thinking: An Overview", various nuances of "planetary thinking" are examined in order to explain why "planetary thinking" nowadays gains a lot of currency. In addition to it, this chapter seeks to uncover and unpack how "planetary thinking" stands integrally proximate to the issues like Illness, New Earth politics and Neoliberal turn, among others. One of the important objectives of this chapter thus is to lay bare "epistemological openings" in the contemporary figurations of "planetary thinking". The second chapter, "Theorizing 'Plasti(e)cological Thinking': Bio-Geo-Eco-At(os)mosis", engages readers with the theoretical strands of "plasti(e)cological thinking" taking bio-geo-eco-at(os)mosis into account in order to spell out its operative logic. This chapter aims at grounding the notion of "plasti(e)cological thinking" in the context of bio-geo-eco-at(os)mosis—a sort of deterritorialized assemblage that represents the ceaseless becomings of the planet and putting the spotlight on how strands of "plasti(e)cological thinking" are capable of remodelling stratified planetary thinking anew. The third chapter, "Contextualizing 'Plasti(e)cological Thinking': Reading Select Indian Eco-texts", seeks to engage readers with the application of "plasti(e)cological thinking" in select Indian literary narratives, intending to show how "plasti(e)cological thinking" can inform and condition the refashioning of stratified "planetary thinking" in many ways. Finally, the

Conclusion titled "'Zoegraphy': Working out an (infra)structural Geoerotics" first presents critical remarks on the configuration of "molecularity" that stands wedded to the production of the "new" and then it is linked up to the process of an (infra)structural Geoerotics by means of taking the help of bio-geo-eco-semiotics. In short, a poetics of molecularity is epistemized in order to make room for the free workings of an (infra)structural geoerotics, which, in turn, lays bare the immanent chaosophy of "zoegraphical" becoming. This final chapter also calls for a sort of multifractalization of "plasti(e)cological thinking" so that it can finely operate beyond the territorial segmentarities of stratified "planetary thinking".

Notes

1. May Heaven and Earth, the Mighty Pair, bedew for us our sacrifice,
    And feed us full with nourishments. (1.22.13, Griffith 12)
This hymn suggests how Vedic sages were very much clear about the co-presences of both Heaven and the Earth. They understood the exteriority of the Earth as distinct from the peripherality of Heaven.

2. In *Ecology: A Textbook*, Hermann Remmert contends that the epistemic terrain of ecology ". . . is concerned with the cycling of matter and the flow of energy, with the way ecosystems function, and with questions of the stability and elasticity of ecosystems" (2) and subsequently, suggests its complex and nuanced functioning through densely mediated ecosystems.

3. In "Brown", Steve Mentz dwells on the emergence of "Brown ecology" and its intersectional connection with the becomings of the Earth:

Thinking brown pushes us into hybrid spaces that span living and nonliving matter, aesthetic values and biological drives. . . . Brown is the color of intimate and uncomfortable contact between human bodies and the non-human world. . . . To be ecological is to be brown, disturbingly. [Brown] . . . is the color on which all agricultural societies, which is to say, all human societies, depend, no matter how green our environmental fantasies. Down in the muck, life is a brown business. (193-194)

4. In "Violate-Black", Stacy Alaimo expresses her deep concerns about atrocious and vicious impacts of human developments in the fields of industry, mining and corporate capitalism: "
. . . scientists and environmentalists warn of the devastating ecological effects of ocean acidification, massive overfishing, bottom trawling, deep-sea mining, shark finning, and decades of dumping toxic and radioactive waste into the oceans" (235). It is by exposing the potentials risks to the ocean, she calls for paying adequate attention to violate-black ecology which ". . . hovers in the bathypelagic, abyssopelagic, and hadal zones, the three regions of the deep seas, one thousand meters down and much deeper, where sunlight cannot descend" (233).

5. Sam Solnick is one important thinker who draws on the layered connections between ecopoetry and climate change in *Poetry and the Anthropocene Ecology, biology and technology in contemporary British and Irish poetry.* "It constructs a highly complex picture of planetary ecology, typified by unpredictable feedback loops which regulate climate, providing suitable conditions for the flourishing of life but, crucially, not necessarily for life on Earth as it currently manifests itself" (128). It may lead one to figure out how different facets of climate change could be analyzed with the help of Ecopoetics.

6. In "Introduction: The Region of the Song", Sharon Lattig shrewdly extends Ecopoetics to the realm of cognition and contends: ". . . a poetic forging and foregrounding of connection must be effected in part cognitively" (1), thereby pointing at the epistemic deterritorialization of Ecopoetics.

Works Cited

Alaimo, Stacy. "Violate-Black." *Prismatic Ecology: Ecotheory beyond Green*, edited by Jeffrey Jerome Cohen, 2013, pp. 233-251.

Bignall, Simon, and Rosi Braidotti. "Posthuman Systems." *Posthuman Ecologies: Complexity and Process after Deleuze*, edited by Braidotti and Bignall, Rowman and Littlefield, 2019, pp. 1-16.

Bryson, J. Scott. Preface. *The West Side of Any Mountain: Place, Space, and Ecopoetry*, by Bryson, University of Iowa Press, 2005, pp. 1-6.

Campos, Isabel Sobral. "Introduction Transnational Ecopoetics." *Ecopoetics and the Global Landscape: Critical Essays*, edited by Campos, Lexington Books, 2019, pp. ix-xvii.

Chakrabarty, Dipesh. *The Climate of History in a Planetary Age.* The University of Chicago Press, 2021.

Cohen, Tom. "The Angel and the Storm 'Material Spirit' in the Era of Climate Change." *Material Spirit Religion and Literature Intranscendent*, edited by Gregory C. Stallings, Manuel Asensi, and Carl Good, Fordham University Press, 2014, pp. 129-153.

Conley, Verena Andermatt. *Ecopolitics: The environment in poststructuralist thought.* Routledge, 2006.

Evernden, Neil. "Beyond Ecology: SELF, PLACE, AND THE PATHETIC FALLACY." *The Ecocriticism Reader: Landmark in Literary Ecology*, edited by Glotfelty and Harold Fromm, The University of Georgia Press, 1996, pp. 102-103.

Garrard, Greg. *Ecocriticism.* Routledge, 2004.

Ghosh, Ranjan. "Globing the Earth: The New Eco-logics of Nature." *SubStance*, vol. 41, no. 1, 2012, pp. 3-14.

Glotfelty, Cheryll. Introduction: Literary Studies in an Age of Environmental Crisis. *The Ecocriticism Reader: Landmark in Literary Ecology*, edited by Glotfelty and Harold Fromm, The University of Georgia Press, 1996, pp. xv-xxxvii.

Griffith, Ralph T. H, translator. *The Hymns of the Ṛgveda.* Motilal Banarsidass, 1896.

Guattari, Felix. *The Three Ecologies*. Translated by Ian Pindar and Paul Sutton, The Athlone Press, 2000.

–. *Schizoanalytic Cartographies*. Translated by Andrew Goffey, Bloomsbury, 2013.

Hengel, Louis van den. "Zoegraphy: Per/forming Posthuman Lives." *Biography*, vol. 35, no. 1, 2012, pp.1-20. https://muse.jhu.edu/article/480240.

Herzogenrath, Bernd. "White." *Prismatic Ecology: Ecotheory beyond Green*, edited by Jeffrey Jerome Cohen, 2013, pp. 1-21.

Knickerbocker, Scott. "Introduction: The Language of Nature, the Nature of Language." *Ecopoetics: The Language of Nature, the Nature of Language*, by Knickerbocker, University of Massachusetts Press, 2012, pp. 1-18.

Kuppers, Petra. *Eco Soma: Pain and Joy in Speculative Performance Encounters*. University of Minnesota Press, 2022.

Lattig, Sharon. "Introduction: The Region of the Song." *Cognitive Ecopoetics A New Theory of Lyric*, by Lattig, Bloomsbury Academic, 2021, pp.1-32.

Magrane, Eric, et al. *Geopeotics in Practice*. Routledge, 2020.

Mentz, Steve. "Brown." *Prismatic Ecology: Ecotheory beyond Green*, edited by Jeffrey Jerome Cohen, 2013, pp. 193-212. Merriam-Webster. Springfield, 1831.

Morton, Timothy. *Ecology Without Nature: Rethinking Environmental Aesthetics*. Harvard University Press, 2007.

–. "Coexistence and Coexistents: Ecology without a World." *Ecocritical Theory: New European Approaches*, edited by Axel Goodbody and Kate Rigby, University of Virginia Press, 2011, pp. 168-180.

Nolan, Sarah. "Un-natural Ecopoetics Natural/Cultural Intersections in Poetic Language and Form." *New International Voices in Ecocriticism*, edited by Serpil Oppermann, Lexington Books, 2015, pp. 87-99.

Oppermann, Serpil. "Introduction New International Voices in Ecocriticism." *New International Voices in Ecocriticism*, edited by Oppermann, Lexington Books, 2015, pp. 1-24.

Philips, Dana. "Is Nature Necessary?" *The Ecocriticism Reader: Landmark in Literary Ecology*, edited by Glotfelty and Harold Fromm, The University of Georgia Press, 1996, pp. 204-224.

Rajan, Chandra, translator. *Kālidāsa: The Loom of Time*. Penguin Books, 1999.

Remmert, Hermann. *Ecology: A Textbook*. Springer-Verlag, 1980.

Rigby, Kate. "Ecopoetics." *Keywords for Environmental Studies*, edited by Joni Adamson, William A. Gleason, and David N. Pellow, New York University Press, 2016, pp. 79-81.

Rueckert, William. "Literature and Ecology: An Experiment in Ecocriticism." *The Ecocriticism Reader: Landmark in Literary Ecology*, edited by Glotfelty and Harold Fromm, The University of Georgia Press, 1996, pp. 105-123.

Sanders, Scott Russell. "Speaking a Word for Nature." *The Ecocriticism Reader: Landmark in Literary Ecology*, edited by Glotfelty and Harold Fromm, The University of Georgia Press, 1996, pp. 182-195.

Solnick, Sam. *Poetry and the Anthropocene Ecology, biology and technology in contemporary British and Irish poetry.* Routledge, 2017.

Soper, Kate. "Representing Nature." *NATURE PROSPECTS,* vol. 9, no. 4, 1998, pp. 61-65. https://doi.org/10.1080/10455759809358833.

Chapter 1

Theoretical "Turns" to Stratified Planetary Thinking: An Overview

Planetary thinking has been in vogue since time immemorial but the figurations of planetary thinking, spread across different spatio-temporal locales, are quite diverse and hence interesting. Following the neoliberal advancements of technology coupled with rapidly changing climatic conditions of the Earth, owing to the serious and massive damages done to existing earthly structures by a section of insensible and greedy people, critical thinkers nowadays put insistence on the re-engagement with planetary thinking in order to figure out how the planet Earth stands at risk and what measures sensible human beings can take up to safeguard the Earth from getting damaged further. Critical re-engagement with planetary thinking could therefore be productive in elucidating the strengths and limits of planetary thinking as far as the restoration of good health of the planet Earth is concerned. It is broadly contended that although planetary thinking at times seems to be a feasible way out to deal with catastrophic climatic changes, it ultimately fails to be an unwavering and effective epistemological instrument to wrestle with the vicious corollaries of climate change, following its gradual leanings to the snares of stratification.

This chapter seeks to unpack critical and theoretical "turns" to planetarity in general and particularly to lay emphasis on how planetary thinking has been developing in conformity with the continuous transformations of the planet. In other words, it is by working out some theoretical frameworks, the nuances of planetary thinking are intended to be mapped in order to help readers figure out how planetary consciousness stands wedded to the tenets of critical thinking, thereby showing relevance and effectiveness of planetary thinking in a moment when the world slips into post-anthropocentric dialecticism. In doing so, this chapter aims at making an overview of planetary thinking which has so much in store and can effectively and potentially radicalize our ways of understanding the differential processuality of the planet Earth in particular. Finally, the limits of stratified planetary thinking are brought out to lay down the ground ready for unfolding "plasti(e)cological thinking" in the following chapter.

Planetary Thinking Then

To be human is to be intended toward the other. . . . Planet-thought opens up to embrace an inexhaustible taxonomy of such names, including but not identical with the whole range of human universals. . . . If we imagine ourselves as planetary subjects rather than global agents, planetary creatures rather than global entities, alterity remains underived from us; it is not our dialectical negation, it contains us as much as it flings us away. (Spivak 73)

Earth System Science (ESS), the science that among other things explains planetary warming and cooling, gives humans a very long, multilayered, and heterotemporal past by placing them at the conjuncture of three (and now variously interdependent) histories whose events are defined by very different timescales: the history of the planet, the history of life on the planet, and the history of the globe made by the logics of empires, capital, and technology. ("The Planet: An Emergent Humanist Category", Chakraborty 1)

The tradition of planetary thinking could be traced back to the ancient past when the world stood divested of both advanced communicative gadgets and transport systems across the world. The ancient figuration of planetary thinking was quite different and was integrally coupled with ritualistic activities in particular. The history of "Planet-thought" could be traced back to ancient times and was very much in compliance with the emergence of the planet as a "humanist category". Here, one may take a stop and ponder over some unsettling questions: did ancient people have a different understanding of the planet from that of the Earth? How did planetary consciousness impact the fashioning and refashioning of society at large? In order to find answers to these questions, one may go back to *Ṛgveda* which documents Vedic formulation of planetarity in terms of ritualism and geo-thinking, immanence and mediation, externalization and exteriority. At first, it needs to be mentioned that Vedic sages first propounded the notion of "dvyāpṛithibi" which refers to both the Heaven and the Earth at a go and then they attempted to deify it so that it can come to their rescue. What is interesting is that even in Vedic times, sages could conceptualize the exteriority of the planet in terms of strata and territories–"duloka" (possibly referring to the distant Heaven) and "vūloka" (referring to the Earth):

I bend the bow for Rudra that his arrow may strike and slay the hater of devotion.

I rouse and order battle for the people, and I have penetrated Earth and Heaven. (10.125.6, Griffith 489)
On the world's summit I bring forth the Father: my home is in the waters, in the ocean.
Thence I extend o'er all existing creatures, and touch even yonder heaven with my forehead. (10.125.7, Griffith 489)
I breathe a strong breath like the wind and tempest, the while I hold together all existence.
Beyond this wide earth and beyond the heavens I have become so mighty in my grandeur. (10.125.8, Griffith 489)

These cited Vedic hymns point to the fact that Vedic sages had a clear understanding of the periphery of the Earth and its integral constituents. They could take the measure of the expansiveness and enormity of the earth by means of considering spatio-temporal aspects. They could also, to some extent, figure out the presence of an external sphere which stays out of the Earth's surface and it, to an extent, speaks of their planetary consciousness. One may be reminded of a few more Vedic hymns which lay bare some other interesting takes on planetarity:

Dhatar, the great Creator, then formed in due order Sun and Moon.
He formed in order Heaven and Earth, the regions of the air, and light. (10.190.3, Griffith 505)
The fifteen lauds are in a thousand places that is as vast as heaven and earth in measure.
A thousand spots contain the mighty thousand. Vak spreadeth forth as far as Prayer extendeth. (10.114.8, Griffith 484)
Indra hath evermore possessed surpassing power: he forced, far from each other, heaven and earth apart.
He hurled impetuous down his iron thunderbolt, a joy to Varuna's and Mitra's worshipper. (10.113.5, Griffith 483)
We call upon the Sage with holy verses, Agni Vaisvanara the ever-beaming,
Who hath surpassed both heaven and earth in greatness: lie is a God below, a God above us. (10.88.14, Griffith 468)
MIGHTY are ye, and far-extended, Heaven and Earth: both Worlds are evermore to us like two young Dames.
Guard us thereby from stronger foe; guard us hereby to give us strength. (10.93.1, Griffith 471)

These Vedic hymns reveal a number of important dimensions that are essentially connected with planetary consciousness. For example, cosmological understanding of the Earth stands embedded in the Vedic notion of planetarity which is also grounded in geological networks of energy and in divinity. What is significant is that they used to interpret the planet in terms of vastness, magnitude, femininity and ritualism. It was quite clear to Vedic sages that planetary consciousness was required to maintain geological, religious, cultural, political and ecological equilibriums and therefore it was put in dialogue with humanism. Deification of "dvyāpṛithibi" was deliberately intended to weave planetary consciousness together with ritualistic emancipation and theodicy. Categorical understanding of the planet in terms of strata and territories was not meant to devise ways of exploiting planetary resources available across the Earth but was thoughtfully carried out to integrate the concept of planetarity with the geological transformations of the Earth.

Planetary consciousness of Vedic sages finds reflections in understanding how the sun's rays play an instrumental role in enlightening the moon; how the movements of the sun result in the happening of the days and nights; how the solar eclipse takes place and in conceptualizing the axis of the planet earth:

> Then verily they recognized the essential form of Tvastar's Bull,
> Here in the mansion of the Moon. (1.84.15, Griffith 45)
> The same in form to-day, the same tomorrow, they still keep Varuna's
> eternal statute. Blameless, in turn they traverse thirty regions, and dart
> across the spirit in a moment. (1.123.8, Griffith 68)
> I will send forth my songs in flow unceasing, like water from the ocean's
> depth, to Indra. Who to his car on both its sides securely hath fixed the
> earth and heaven as with an axle. (10.89.4, Griffith 468)

It suggests that Vedic planetary consciousness was not restricted to certain fields of activity. Rather, it stood mediated in the astronomical understanding of the planet as well. Cited Vedic hymns also indicate how Vedic sages used to engage themselves linking the notion of planetarity up with the material transformations of the planet observed through astronomical alterations. It strikes one to wonder the way Vedic sages could figure out the existence of the axis of the earth without taking resort to any modern scientific gadget. Advancements in the domain of planetarity in terms of astronomical measurements seem worth considering because they actually laid the foundation for posterity to take up "planetary thinking" further.

Interestingly, Vedic notion of "planetary thinking" was grounded in the intersections between corporeality and ritualism so much so that in addition to the deification of "dvyāpṛithibi", its distinctive physical appearance was used to be comprehended by means of dawn, night, territorial expansiveness and balanced structure:

> THERE are the Dawn and Night, the grand and beauteous Pair, Earth, Heaven, and Varuna, Mitra, and Aryaman.
> Indra I call, the Maruts, Mountains, and the Floods, Adityas, Heaven and Earth, the Waters, and the Sky. (10.36.1, Griffith 438)

It suggests that Vedic notion of planetarity got sprung out of the intensive and extensive becomings of the Earth. Vedic sages had a clear understanding of the limits of the sky, the earth and the atmosphere–the sum-total of which could not exceed the might and greatness of Indra:

> To him, to Indra, when he slew the Dragon, the Dames, too, Consorts of the Goda, wove praises.
> The mighty heaven and earth hath he encompassed: thy greatness heaven and earth, combined, exceed not. (1.61.8, Griffith 35)

This Vedic hymn attests to the fact that Vedic notion of "planetary thinking" was fully steeped in religiosity and was instrumental in inspiring the posterity to take up different nuances of planetarity although the term was not in vogue. Vedic "planetary thinking" was extended to giving adequate importance to the sun which happens to be the source of energy and light and is responsible for warming the earth. Modern sciences inform us that the sunrays partake in diffident kinds of chemical and organic reactions and end up producing the earth greener:

> THE brilliant presence of the Gods hath risen, the eye of Mitra, Varuna and Agni.
> The soul of all that moveth not or moveth, the Sun hath filled the air and earth and heaven. (1.115.1, Griffith 62)

It vouches for the multifacetedness of Vedic "planetary thinking" which was quite well ahead of its time.

Vedic "planetary thinking" was also predicated upon the origin and developments of the universe. Vedic sages engaged themselves in mulling over some cosmological questions which, in turn, laid the ground ready for Vedic notion of planetarity to flourish. Some of the important cosmological questions embedded in Vedic hymns are referred to bring out the connections between planetarity and cosmology:

> THEN was not non-existent nor existent: there was no realm of air, no sky beyond it.
> What covered in, and where? and what gave shelter? Was water there, unfathomed depth of water? (10.129.1, Griffith 490)
> Darkness there was: at first concealed in dark new this All was indiscriminated chaos.
> All that existed then was void and form less: by the great power of Warmth was born that Unit. (10.129.3, Griffith 490)
> Who verily knows and who can here declare it, whence it was born and whence comes this creation?
> The Gods are later than this world's production. Who knows then whence it first came into being? (10.129.6, Griffith 490)
> He, the first origin of this creation, whether he formed it all or did not form it, Whose eye controls this world in highest heaven, he verily knows it, or perhaps he knows not. (10.129.7, Griffith 490)

These Vedic hymns clearly reflect that Vedic formulation of "planetary thinking" stood enmeshed with cosmological thoughts and was explicitly well-advanced for its time. Diversities within Vedic "planetary thinking" also suggest that Vedic sages could understand that it was profoundly important to approach the planet from multiple standpoints simply because the crux of planetarity cuts across all earthly entities. They also thought of including "temporality" and "spatiality" in problematizing the notion of "planetarity" and engaged themselves in exploring some open questions–a trend in "planetary thinking" which is nowadays being employed by contemporary string theorists. Rightly has Michael D. Lemonick contended in "Before the Big Bang":

> The hidden dimensions and colliding worlds in the new model are an outgrowth of superstring theory, an increasingly popular concept in fundamental physics. . . . In order to make it work, theorists have to assume that space isn't merely three-dimensional, the way it appears to our puny human senses, but rather that it has up to 10 spatial dimensions. Just as a bedsheet hanging on a clothesline appears to be a two-dimensional object hanging in a three-dimensional world, all of space-time would be suspended in a higher-order space. In keeping with this two-dimensional analogy, string theorists describe our observable

universe as a membrane –"brane" for short – flapping in the breezes of the actual 10-dimensional cosmos. (2004, no. pag.)

Although Vedic nāsadíya hymns do not offer conclusive answers to the origin of the universe but bring out the fact that open-ended cosmological questions circumstanced by the strands of planetarity need to be instrumentalized to keep on exploring the genesis of the universe. String theorists are in particular interested in spelling out the cosmological singularity which is supposed to have laid down the ground for the birth of the planet. Although there are a number of conceptual dichotomies between Vedic scientific thoughts and that of string theory, Vedic cosmological questions seem to be capable of providing clues to contemporary string theorists in addressing the open-ended questions in a comprehensive manner. The essence of Vedic notion of "planetary think-ing" is perhaps best captured in the following Vedic hymn:

> A hymn of prayer and praise to Prithivī or deified Earth
> Truth, high and potent Law, the Consecrating Rite, Fervour,
> Brahma, and Sacrifice uphold the Earth.
> May she, the Queen of all that is and is to be, may Prithivī
> make ample space and room for us. (12.1.1, *The Hymns of the Athar-*
> *vaveda*, Griffith 350)

It puts the spotlight on the importance of "truth", "potent law" and "fervour"– all of which work together in adding up more nuances to the Vedic notion of "planetary thinking". It is also suggestive of how different figurations of "life" on the planet Earth can be elevated to the status of greatness by means of em-bracing all the mentioned factors together.

Planetary Thinking Now

With the advancements of informational technology followed by the rapid dis-semination of commercial exchanges across the world in the 1990s onwards, the Earth witnessed rapid human progressions which, albeit, are uneven and heterogeneous in terms of manifestation and potency. Setting up of eco-un-friendly projects backed up by global connectivity in terms of post-globalizational discourses renders the earth vulnerable to speedy destruction. Put in other words, developed countries set up profiteering yet not-so-eco-friendly projects, which impacts the planet earth. Millennium Ecosystem As-sessment (MEA) published in 2005 clearly draws one's attention to the way human beings have collectively altered the material histories of the earth: "Over the past 50 years, humans have changed ecosystems more rapidly and extensively than in any comparable period of time in human history, largely to meet rapidly growing demands for food, fresh water, timber, fiber and fuel. This has resulted in a substantial and largely irreversible loss in the diversity of life on Earth" (no. pag.). This suggests that Scientists are also of this viewpoint that it is because of the massive human developments and advancements, the earth nowadays stands at risk and it is the need of the hour to think of the planet taking recourse to interdisciplinary perspectives. Different ecological movements have already taken place across the world but these have not produced significant outcomes in altering the conditions of the planet. Ronald A. T. Judy is one thinker who strikingly argues in "Provisional Note on Formations of Planetary Violence": ". . . the challenge is to try seriously and rigorously to take up the question, who could act for the human in these circumstances and how?" (150). Judy means to say that it is urgently important to take up the issue of human-led violence on the planet because the well-being of the planet earth is consequent upon the containment of human-led violence. In other words, following Judy's contention, one may argue that contemporary "planetary thinking" cannot but incorporate the issue of violence as it seems to be quite vicious to the ontic dimensions of the planet.

The concept of contemporary "planetary thinking" stands tied to ecopedagogy which, in the words of Richard Kahn, ". . . seeks to interpolate quintessentially Freirian aims of the humanization of experience and the achievement of a just and free world with a future-oriented ecological politics that militantly opposes the globalization of neoliberalism and imperialism, on the one hand, and attempts to foment collective ecoliteracy and realize culturally relevant forms of knowledge grounded in normative concepts such as sustainability, planetarity, and biophilia, on the other" (18). Kahn has rightly argued that pedagogical methods could be employed to stretch the limit of contemporary "planetary thinking" in that ecoliteracy needs to be worked out among the inhabitants of the planet so that they pull themselves back from exploiting the planet for anthropocentric purposes. As this planet stands as much for the human world as it is for the non-human world, eco-literary consciousness can be held effective in dismantling oppressive and repressive structures working against the planet. In short, eco-literary dimensions can further open up the domain of contemporary "planetary thinking".

Contemporary brand of "planetary thinking" takes into account human-induced "slow violence" against Nature, which is backed up by the flows of global capitalism. In a way, epistemological strands of "planetarity" get sprung out of a post-globalization scenario where economic power remains centralized within a "few" and a majority of poor people are forced to indulge in different kinds of eco-unfriendly activities. These complex power dynamics get functional support from marginalized men and women who can neither refuse the offers of employment in different capitalistic and vicious enterprises nor can earn their daily livelihoods. Thus, rightly has Ranjan Ghosh pointed out in "Globing the Earth: The New Eco-logics of Nature" that "green globality" is not just only productive of "green anxiety" but also pushes "planetary dimensions" to reduce ". . . eco-negotiations to a dialogue between the 'powerful few' and the 'disempowered many'" (6). Ghosh is possibly worried about the way rapid advancements of technology do not let "green space" operate through it and unfortunately, are vicious to the free run of ecological intensities. Ghosh adds up: ". . . complex monologics of green space can easily operate through technocratic expertise, which, representing particular interests, develops its own mode of production and dissemination of knowledge" (6). Ghosh's observation unsettles hackneyed ways of making inroads into the interface between ecology and technology and suggests how eco-logics get folded into the contemporary conceptualizations of "planetarity". It means that planetary thinking today leads one to engage himself in examining the nuanced interactions between ecology and technology, which constitutes important strands of "planetarity".

It is because of the heavy application of technology, different constituting components of the planet Earth are at risk. In order to extract maximum resources out of the earth's abundance, human beings cleverly make use of technology but do not keep it mind that reckless and careless use of technology might be quite vicious to the earth. Global warming is a constant threat nowadays and different protocols have been set up to bring it under check but unfortunately, dire and dreadful conditions rendered by global warming continue to persist on the planet earth and so many marine and terrestrial species are facing the threat of extinction. Misuse or overuse of technology directly impacts the climatic conditions of the earth and every inhabitant of the earth has to bear with it. Therefore, declining climatic conditions of the earth get included in contemporary planetary thinking inasmuch as the climate happens to be integrally connected to the exteriority of the planet earth. Rightly has Andrew P. Ingersoll brought out in *Planetary Climates* that planetary liminality of the earth could be figured out if one posits the earth in contrast with the larger planetary system of which it is a part and parcel:

> Earth has a wide range of climates, but the range among the planets is much greater. Studying the climates of other planets helps us understand the basic physical processes in a larger context. . . . Earth is the only planet with water in all three phases– solid, liquid, and gas. Mars

has plenty of water, but it's almost all locked up in the polar caps as ice. There's a small amount of water vapor in its atmosphere but no standing bodies of liquid water. Venus has a small amount of water vapor in its atmosphere, but the Venus surface is hot enough to melt lead and is too hot for solid or liquid water. Thus by human standards, Venus is too hot and Mars is too cold. The classic "habitable zone," where Earth resides and life evolved, lies in between. (1)

Taking Ingersoll's contention into account, one may tenably put forward that conditions pertaining to the climatic specificities of the earth need to be unearthed so as to lay out the role of planetary liminality in maintaining ecological *status quo* of the planet earth. The idea of planetarity liminality of the earth can facilitate one to understand how the earth stands inclusive of human and non-human ecologies–the co-existence of different kinds of ecology in actuality stands grounded in the geology of the planetary liminality. In a nutshell, planetarity liminality lays down an epistemological framework that is required to delve deeper into the "ontical" and ontological dimensions of the earth.

Contemporary "planetary thinking" is also in dialogue with "waste studies", for the latter plays an instrumental role in striking a balance between different kinds of planetary ecology. Waste theorists are of the view that ". . . humans play in generating, ignoring, coping with, and analyzing waste in its various manifestations" (Morrison 7). It means that waste is not a matter of impotence; rather is very much a literary category which can help one figure out the world around us afresh. Close examinations of different kinds of waste include their distinctive production process, innate narrativity and hidden metaphysics. In *The Literature of Waste Material Ecopoetics and Ethical Matter*, Susan Signe Morrison offers some relevant insights on the distinct figurations and configurations of "waste" in the following terms:

> Waste necessarily implicates history, and implies materiality, metaphor, and emotional affect. Though waste has been understood differently in various places over time, certain aspects remain constant: waste is always material (first) and figurative and metaphoric (second). Without the material that is discarded, we cannot enter the realm of the metaphoric, of literature, and of the imagination. Waste is literal and literary. Indeed, "matter itself becomes a text" or a "site of narrativity." The meaning of waste "exceeds interpretation," and is "radically litteral [sic] in that it always derives from the residue of waste which resists quick degradation." (8)

Morrison means to suggest that waste is at once a materiality and at times bears metaphorical nuances, for it both comes off and ends up in "waste". Keeping this argument in mind, it can be put forward that "planetary wastes", too, need to be investigated critically because it at once impacts the transformability of the planet earth and can provide relevant insights in constructing ecopedagogical frameworks so as to keep planetary risks at bay. Epistemic integration of contemporary planetary thinking with waste studies seems to be productive in the sense that deposition, circulation, dissemination and mineralization of waste regulate the mediated and nuanced becomings of planetary ecologies. Slavoj Žižek thus reminds us in *Living in the End Times*: "The properly aesthetic attitude of a radical ecologist is not that of admiring or longing for a pristine nature of virgin forests and clear sky, but rather that of accepting waste as such, of discovering the aesthetic potential of waste, of decay, of the inertia of rotten material which serves no purpose" (35). Following Žižek's insight, it can be contended that incorporation of the materiality and metaphoricality of waste both extends the horizon of contemporary "planetary thinking" and whets the effectuality of it as an epistemic instrument for critical inquiry.

In "Introduction: The Planetary Condition", Amy J. Elias and Christian Moraru work out critico-theoretical underpinnings of planetarity in connection with post-globalism and post-postmodernity. They contend: ". . . [the] discourse of planetarity presents itself, in response to the twenty-first-century world and to the decreasing ability of the postmodern theoretical apparatus to account for it, as a new structure of awareness, as a methodical receptivity to the geothematics of planetariness characteristic of a fast-expanding series of cultural formations" (xi). What it suggests is that their formulation of planetarity does not conform to the governing principles of globalism but it stands rooted in the logic of "*relationality*"– ". . . an ethicization of the ecumenic process of coming together or 'worlding'" (xii). It calls for an epistemic deterritorialization and destratification of "planetarity" which is often territorialized and codified within the bounds of spatio-temporality, materiality, abstraction and homogenization.

Destratifying Planetarity:
Differentiality, Diagram and Supple Segmentarity

It is now clear that discursive attempts have been made to codify planetarity in different epistemic fashions but it seems to be profoundly important to trace differential intensities of planetarity, which is influenced by onticological factors, transgresses spatio-temporal limits and has been evolving in consummate with political, cultural, ecological, pedagogical, economical, and technological changes. One may easily find that the concept of planetarity is fraught with strata and territories, which in turn refrains one from grasping its intensive and extensive differentiality. Instead of pinning planetarity down in certain epistemic presuppositions, the concept of planetarity has to be opened up so as to let people understand how the epistemization of planetarity stands as much fluid and transgressive as its material counterpart and thus it can tenably be subjected to what Deleuze and Guattari articulate as "destratification". In *A Thousand Plateaus: Capitalism and Schizophrenia*, Gilles Deleuze and Felix Guattari reflect: "Continuum of intensities, combined emission of particles or signs-particles, conjunction of deterritorialized flows: these are the three factors proper to the plane of consistency; they are brought about by the abstract machine and are constitutive of destratification" (70). Keeping this argument in mind, one may argue that planetarity in actuality consists of "continuum of intensities, combined emission of particles or signs-particles, conjunction of deterritorialized flows" and therefore, cannot be restricted within the patterns of stratification. Forces of deterritorialization inscribed in planetarity do not allow it to get locked up in tangles of territorialization. In other words, the intensive differentiality of planetarity backed up by free intensities accounts for the fluid ontology of planetarity. Destratifying planetarity entails the operationalization of what Deleuze and Guattari call "assemblage" which stands embedded in the concept of "machine". In *ARTMACHINES: Deleuze, Guattari, Simondon*, Anne Sauvagnargues reflects: ". . . [the] concept of the machine thus defines a historical and social machinic assemblage, an assemblage of enunciation, and a machinic assemblage of bodies, which concerns the operativity of singular social functioning" (187). Sauvagnargues means to say that the concept of the machine is "social before being technical" (187) and is the guiding principle for actualization of assemblage. Planetarity is replete with a series of assemblages–interconnected operations which help it transgress the bounds of codification. Machinic operations of planetarity through political, cultural and social installations can be deciphered if one considers differential becomings of planetarity.

Destratification of planetarity includes consideration of infrastructure as an epistemic category. Critical engagement with planetarity pushes one to take into account infrastructural viewpoints which are capable of exposing how the interiority of planetarity is grounded in an invisible structure. Deleuzo-Guattarian formulation of "diagram" can be employed to examine how planetarity stands wedded to the "lines of flight". In *A Thousand Plateaus: Capitalism and Schizophrenia*, Deleuze and Guattari contend:

> For a true abstract machine pertains to an assemblage in its entirety: it
> is defined as the diagram of that assemblage. It is not language based
> but diagrammatic and superlinear. (91)
> Destratify, open up to a new function, a diagrammatic function. (134)
> . . . [the] diagrammatic or abstract machine does not function to repre-
> sent, even something real, but rather constructs a real that is yet to
> come, a new type of reality. (142)

Following these critical insights, it can be put forward that planetarity assumes
diagrammatic trajectories to evade the snares of territorialization and can
hardly be deciphered in terms of certain epistemic predispositions because
planetarity is devoid of any fixed and inflexible structure. Planetarity is a "Mat-
ter-Function" (*A Thousand Plateaus*, Deleuze and Guattari 141) which follows
diagrammatic pathways in the process of becoming and has its own micropolitics. It suggests that planetarity is made up of "molecular lines" that "bring
everything into play"–a micropolitical engagement with which can help one
reveal that the concept of planetarity is always already linked up with "the production of the new" and thus does not end up in rigid segmentarity. Deleuze
and Guattari opine:

> It is not enough, therefore, to oppose the centralized to the segmentary.
> Nor is it enough to oppose two kinds of segmentarity, one supple and
> primitive, the other modern and rigidified. (*A Thousand Plateaus* 213)

They are of this viewpoint that whereas rigid segmentarity is indicative of a territorial machine, supple segmentarity carries the suggestion of deterritorial
becomings which indeed characterize the notion of planetarity.

Micropolitical engagement with the notion of planetarity brings out how the
signifying intensities which constitute the crux of planetarity rhizomatically
follow "the lines of flight" thereby refraining planetarity from being caught up
in rigid segmentarity. The micropercept of planetarity suggests how "molecular assemblages" embedded in the notion of planetarity lead it to transgress the
bounds of stratification and seek to cut across the mapping of worlding.
Deleuze and Guattari further reflect: "When the machine becomes planetary or
cosmic, there is an increasing tendency for assemblages to miniaturize, to become micro-assemblages" (*A Thousand Plateaus* 215). Following this
contention, one may suggest that destratifying the notion of planetarity results
in the production of micro-assemblages which work at the molecular levels to
help planetarity get past rigid segmentarity. It also reveals how the "zones of
indiscernibility" (*A Thousand Plateaus* 226) in actuality lead planetarity to get

diffused among its signifying intensities. Micropolitical interventions into the notion of planetarity seem to be quite relevant in the era of post-anthropocentrism which puts a lot of emphasis on non-humanistic understanding of the planet Earth in order to neutralize the preponderance of anthropocentric interplay of power politics. Attempts have been made to usurp planetarity in terms of coding and overcoding but the process of destratification drives planetarity to the "Plane of Consistency" or a "Plane of Immanence". It can also cater to new insights in the domain of planetary thinking in that instead of pushing critical thinkers to comply with conventional ways of knowing the planet Earth, it encourages them to figure out distinctive micropolitics and micropercept of planetarity. In short, the domain of planetarity opens up a corpuscular spatiality which can hardly be divided into strata and territories and stands in the state of becoming.

Planetary Illness, New Earth and the Logic of Global Capitalism

Destratifying "planetarity" does not only bring out its fluid molecular configuration induced by the intersecting trajectories of its constitutive elements but also exposes how planetarity stands exposed to the buffets of illness perpetuated by human atrocities of different sorts. It is because of human interventions into the geology of the Earth, the latter becomes affected by a number of illnesses. Climate change happens to be one of the important illnesses that the planet Earth suffers nowadays a lot and it pushes critical thinkers to take into account the dire and dreadful impinges of climatic catastrophe on the planet Earth. In a seminal article "A New Earth: Deleuze and Guattari in the Anthropocene", Arun Saldanha and Hannah Stark cogently reflect:

> The Anthropocene is the geological age in which human impact on earth systems has become irreversible and will be detectable far into the future. It is therefore the greatest challenge currently facing life on earth. Its effects are omnipresent: ocean acidification, deforestation, the loss of species diversity through extinction, changes to the earth's surface due to population migration and alterations to geomorphology, global warming and much more. Describing these changes as indicators of a new geological epoch acknowledges the unprecedented and planetary magnitude of human impact on the earth's ecosystems and geochemistry. (428)

Saldanha and Stark rightly argue that the Anthropocene wrecks havoc on the planet and the indelible marks of human activity on the planet are supposed to impact the course of futurity. In a way, human beings are quite responsible for changing the ontic dimensions of the Earth. Therefore, the concept of "planetary health" nowadays turns out to be an important epistemic category which can both empower "planetary thinking" and expand its purview of it. It is undeniably true that vicious human activities in the garb of illness seep into the molar configuration of planetarity and entail ontical alterations of the Earth. The metaphor of illness is important here in the sense that appalling human actions like mining, geo-engineering, and release of toxic elements into the body of the planet, among others, subtly unsettle and upset the segmentarity of the Earth and renders a territorial entropy. Terrasophical interventions in particular can provide useful insights into examining the conditions of dwindling "planetary health". For example, the notion of terrasophical stratigraphy can be employed to argue that the "planetary health" stands pervasive of human and non-human worlds and the figurations of the planetary ailment stand enmeshed with planetary fitness. Terrasophical stratigraphical insights suggest that planetary illness or planetary ailment stand in connection with its molar counterpart and any sort of human-led vicious activity results in the prominence of planetary ailment. For example, when the level of pollution crosses its permissible limit of tolerance, it starts to impact the transformation of the planet. Human beings always tend to understand "planetary health" in terms of exteriority, but it is important to delve deeper into the interiority of the Earth to understand how violent human activities get precipitated in the form of illness on the folds of the Earth. Moreover, it is with the progression of human civilization, factors determining the conditions of "planetary health" are altering and consequently, it becomes subject to "planetary thinking".

The notion of "planetary coexistence" could be helpful in guiding one to figure out the ways the Earth stands in a crisis. In *Whole Earth Thinking and Planetary Coexistence: Ecological wisdom at the intersection of religion, ecology, and philosophy*, Sam Mickey offers an interesting insight into the challenges of planetary coexistence and how these impact the conditions of planetary healthy:

> To exist on Earth today is to face the challenges of planetary coexistence. . . . Many of today's planetary problems are unprecedented. Humans have never had to figure out what to do with things like plastic, Styrofoam, a globalized economy, or the planet's climate. Challenges of this scale require planetary ways of thinking . . . "whole Earth thinking" . . . [can be employed] as a way of understanding and responding to the challenges of planetary coexistence. (2)

Mickey is clearly pointing at the necessity of "planetary thinking" which can help one effectively deal with the co-extensive becomings of the planet through temporality, topography, spatiality, humanity, non-humanity and so on. The idea of "Earth thinking" reminds one of Deleuze and Guattari's formulation of geophilosophy which explicates how territory and the Earth intersect and interact with each other. In *What is philosophy?* they reflect:

> . . . [Geophilosophical] thinking takes place in the relationship of territory and the earth. . . . Territory and earth are two components with two zones of indiscernibility–deterritorialization (from territory to the earth) and reterritorialization (from earth to territory). (85-86)

Geophilosophical thinking can effectively empower planetary thinking by means of unpacking layered interactions between deterritorialization and reterritorialization. In addition to it, it can lay down frameworks for earth thinking which plays an instrumental role in constructing a New Earth which is capable of maintaining planetary health under control.

It is true that factors involved in determining the health of the planet are important in knowing how planetary thinking is spearheading the birth of the New Earth which has no room for the superiority of the human world over the non-human world. New Earth, in a way, offers a space for the smooth operation of planetary thinking and is very much central to the co-extensive becomings of all materialities. Rightly has Sam Mickey contended in *Whole Earth Thinking and Planetary Coexistence: Ecological wisdom at the intersection of religion, ecology, and philosophy.* "Earth thinking to articulate comprehensive, inclusive, and relevant interpretations of the challenges facing planetary coexistence" (50). Mickey's contention on earth thinking corresponds to what Guattari configured as "ecosophy". Besides it, it can be argued that critical conceptions of the New Earth can provide ways through the planet can be fully taken care of. One may be reminded of the following excerpts which reflect on the enormous significance of "earth thinking" in a moment of planetary crisis:

> These interiorities, once taken into thought, are traumas–with trauma here understood as interiorized exteriority. . . . These traumas plant instabilities within the earth and initiate the internal ungroundings. . . . (Woodard 17-18)
> One need only point to climate change, widespread environmental toxification, the destruction of global biodiversity, and a host of other ills to appreciate that humanity is stretching the world to and beyond ecological limits. Humanity is, through the production of widespread

> environmental harm, in the act of producing what author Bill McKibben
> has called a new "Eaarth"–an Earth 2.0. . . . (Nicholson and Jinnah 1)
> Deleuze and Guattari's call for a new earth is a result of what they see as
> the encroachment of chaos and common sense on our power to think
> about the earth (and the power of the earth to provoke thinking. (Parry
> 126)

These excerpts uncover different nuances of "planetary thinking" and under-
score the differential processuality of the earth. Planetary thinking makes one
aware of how geotrauma, one of the important aspects of planetary health, results in the ungrounding of the earth whose exteriority is forced into its interior
space and the other way round. Human activities entailing geotrauma need to
be brought under check; otherwise, the geotrauma of the earth can get worse
with time. One may take an example to understand how geotrauma stands affective on the plasticity of the planet earth: geo-engineering works like artificial
constructions on the materiality of the earth, destruction of green vegetation
for making room for the expansion of urbanization projects, uses of technology
to exploit the natural productivity of the earth, and so on seek to alter the external terrain of the earth either by means of ungrounding or digging up and it
entails changes in the internal configuration and intensive processuality of the
earth. Contemporary "planetary thinking" thus has to be inclusive of "planetary
coexistence", "planetary health" and climate change. Tinkering "planetarity"
with earth thinking could be useful in laying out the operativity of the New
Earth.

Global capitalist consumptions of the resources of the earth impact the planetary health in many ways. Overuses of the productivity of the earth backed up
by the global circulation of capital make the planet all the more susceptible to
climatic catastrophes. Tim Di Muzio is one important thinker who attempts to
connect global capitalism with carbon emission and how their interactions lay
down the ground for the rise of "planetary thinking" that is required to deal
with planetary health-related issues in *Carbon Capitalism Energy, Social Reproduction and World Order.*

> As carbon capitalism became more institutionalized and organized, this
> was always the result of a fusion of state fiscal and growing corporate
> power. Where greater energy could be harnessed, more elaborate appa-
> ratuses of violence could be constructed and more domination over
> populations and resources could be applied against resistance interna-
> tionally. (115)

Taking resort to Muzio's observation, one may argue that governmental interventions into the exorbitant emission of carbon in the air are needed to help
the planet earth stay healthy. It is arguably true that terrasophical insights need
to be worked out in connection with what Deleuze and Guattari call "ecosophy" to lay down fresh critical frameworks for "planetary thinking" that seems
to play a crucial role in maintaining the health of the planet. In "Ecosophy as
an ethical mode of existence", Mahoro Murasawa and Stéphane Nadaud reflect: ". . . ecosophy is a practical way of thinking, a way of living – put simply,
an ethic" (127). Taking recourse to this insight, it can be argued that terrasophical insights backed up by the logic of "ecosophy" can be turned into a "war
machine" to unsettle and disrupt the marauding march of global capitalism in
the guise of neoliberalism. Neoliberal economic frameworks, in particular, are
responsible for making the global platform ready for the free dissemination of
exploitative mechanisms which are quite vicious and detrimental to the planet
Earth. It subtly opens up g(l)ocal opportunities for exploitation of the productivity of the Earth to those who are driven by the principles of neoliberal
consumerism. Whereas neoliberalism seeks to territorialize productive and
healthy zones of the planet, terrasophical insights in association with "heterogenesis" can work effectively in destabilizing networks of global consumerism.
One may be reminded of the following critical excerpts thereby helping one
understand the efficacy of terrasophy in guiding planetary thinking to revive
the ailing health of the planet:

> Heterogenesis is particularly central to ecosophy where it has an aes-
> thetical–ethical–political meaning as when Guattari concludes The
> Three Ecologies in defining it as 'processes of continuous resingulariza-
> tion. Individuals must become both more united and increasingly
> different'. (Laberge 111)
> . . . the neoliberal state should favour strong individual private property
> rights, the rule of law, and the institutions of freely functioning markets
> and free trade. (Harvey 64)

Therefore, planetary thinking needs to be reworked in such a way that it incorporates the issues and concerns of planetary health which nowadays faces a
number of challenges posed by global capitalism. Considering the continual
becoming(s) of the planet, "geokinetic" insights can well be folded into the traversal trajectories of planetary thinking which aims at deterritorializing
neoliberal ways of exploiting the earth thereby putting its health at risk. Planetary thinking has to be an integrative project which must aim at reviving the

declining conditions of health of the planet by means of actualizing earth thinking.

Works Cited

Chakraborty, Dipesh. "The Planet: An Emergent Humanist Category." *Critical Inquiry*, vol. 46, 2019, pp. 1-31. 00093-1896/19/4601-0002.

Deleuze, Gilles, and Felix Guattari. *What is Philosophy?* Columbia University Press, 1994.

—. *A Thousand Plateaus: Capitalism and Schizophrenia.* University of Minnesota Press, 1987.

Elias, Amy J., and Christian Moraru. "Introduction: The Planetary Condition." *The Planetary Turn Relationality and Geoaesthetics in the Twenty-First Century*, edited by Elias and Moraru, Northwestern University Press, 2015, pp. xi-xxxvii.

Ghosh, Ranjan. "Globing the Earth: The New Eco-logics of Nature." *SubStance*, vol. 41, no. 1, 2012, pp. 3-14. https://doi.org/10.1353/sub.2012.0008

Griffith, Ralph T. H, translator. *The Hymns of the Atharvaveda.* Global Grey Ebooks, 1896.

—, translator. *The Hymns of the Ṛgveda.* Motilal Banarsidass, 1896.

Harvey, David. *A Brief History of Neoliberalism.* Oxford University Press, 2005.

Ingersoll, Andrew P. *Planetary Climates.* Princeton University Press, 2013.

Judy, Ronald A. T. "Provisional Note on Formations of Planetary Violence." *boundary* 2 vol. 33, no. 3, 2006, pp. 141-150. DOI 10.1215/01903659-2006-019.

Kahn, Richard. *Critical Pedagogy, Ecoliteracy, & Planetary Crisis THE ECOPEDAGOGY MOVEMENT.* Peter Lang, 2010.

Laberge, Jean-Sebastien. "Heterogenesis, Ecosophy and Dissent." *Schizoanalysis and Ecosophy: Reading Deleuze and Guattari*, edited by Constantin V. Boundas, Bloomsbury Academic, 2018, pp. 109-127.

Lemonick, Michael D. "Before the Big Bang." *Discover*, Feb 5, 2004. https://www.discovermagazine.com/the-sciences/before-the-big-bang.

Mickey, Sam. *Whole Earth Thinking and Planetary Coexistence: Ecological wisdom at the intersection of religion, ecology, and philosophy.* Routledge, 2016.

Millennium Ecosystem Assessment (MEA). 2005. https://www.millenniumassessment.org/en/index.html. Accessed on Nov. 20, 2021.

Morrison, Susan Signe. *The Literature of Waste Material Ecopoetics and Ethical Matter.* Palgrave Macmillan, 2015.

Murasawa, Mahoro, and Stéphane Nadaud. "Ecosophy as an ethical mode of existence." *Why Guattari? A Liberation of Cartographies, Ecologies and Politics*, edited by Thomas Jellis, Joe Gerlach, and J. D. Dewsbury, Routledge, 2019, pp. 119-132.

Muzio, Tim Di. *Carbon Capitalism: Energy, Social Reproduction and World Order.* Rowman and Littlefield International Ltd., 2015.

Nicholson, Simon, and Sikina Jinnah. "Introduction: Living on a New Earth." *New Earth Politics Essays from the Anthropocene*, edited by, Nicholson and Jinnah, The MIT Press, 2016, pp. 1-16.

Parry, Jason. "Philosophy as Terraforming: Deleuze and Guattari on Designing a New Earth." *Diacritics*, vol. 47, no. 3, 2019, pp. 108-138. https://doi.org/10.1353/dia.2019.0028.

Saldanha, Arun, and Hannah Stark. "A New Earth: Deleuze and Guattari in the Anthropocene." *Deleuze Studies*, vol. 10, no. 4, 2016, pp. 427-439.

Sauvagnargues, Anne. *ARTMACHINES: Deleuze, Guattari, Simondon.* Edinburgh University Press, 2016.

Spivak, Gayatri Chakravorty. *Death of a Discipline.* Columbia University Press, 2003.

Woodard, Ben. *On an Ungrounded Earth: Towards a New Geophilosophy.* Punctum books, 2013.

Žižek, Slavoj. *Living in the End Times.* Verso, 2011.

Chapter 2

Theorizing *Plasti(e)cological Thinking*: Bio-Geo-Eco-At(os)mosis

"The form of thought today . . . is ontologically plastic. . ." (Introduction: Staging Encounters, Bhandar and Goldberg-Hiller 2015, 1)

Even today the public image of plastics is not entirely positive and the significant contribution of plastics to raising the standard of living and quality of life is not fully recognised. (Brydson 11)

Plastic is pretty much everywhere in the world now, stemming from microscopic levels. It's in the air, it's in the soil, it's in the water. That is the reality, borne out of increasing amounts of scientific research documenting our global plastic footprint. (Plamondon and Sinha 12)

At the outset, one may stop and ask: what is "plasti(e)cological thinking"? Therefore, it seems to be useful to begin with a working definition of what "plasti(e)cological thinking" is. "Plasti(e)cological thinking" refers to a kind of epistemological framework which comprises critical insights pertaining to both plasticity and ecology. Detailed investigation of these two terms can help one figure out how these two different notions can be clubbed together to theorize the fundamentals of "plasti(e)cological thinking".

At this point, one may stop and think: what is plasticity? What are the important figurations of plasticity? How does the notion of plasticity help one comprehend the world around us? What is ecology? Does the terrain of ecology need theoretical experimentation? How do the interactions between plasticity and ecology end up in the configuration of "plasti(e)cological thinking"? Where does "plasti(e)cological thinking" lead humanity at large? How does the theoretical experimentation with "plasti(e)cological thinking" cater epistemic interstices to ecocritics? The invention of plastics has brought about revolutionary changes in the world and leaves considerable impacts on almost everything. Sometimes, it is supposed that plastic is actually helpful for humanity because of its durability and longevity. There are others who think that plastic in actuality is vicious and ruinous to the Earth in general, for it has the power to regulate and deregulate deterritorializing movements of the Earth.

Nowadays, the world stands covered up by plastics which impede the natural fluidity and processuality of different Earthly entities. Roland Barthes happens to be a critical thinker who has expatiated on the ontological instability of plastics in *Mythologies*: ". . . plastic . . . is, in essence, the stuff of alchemy . . . the transmutation of matter . . . plastic is the very idea of its infinite transformation. . . . Plastic remains impregnated throughout with this wonder: it is less a thing than the trace of a movement" (97). Barthes is quite right in arguing that plastic is an intriguing entity which gets governed by its own self-sustaining transformability. It is malleable, supple and pliable in nature. Plastics can take up shapes at their disposal and more interestingly, plastics do not get settled down in any particular form. The intrusion of plastics into anthropogenic activities results in "ontological" and "ontical" changes in the Earth. Barthes anticipates in advance:

> Plastic is wholly swallowed up in the fact of being used: ultimately, objects will be invented for the sole pleasure of using them. The hierarchy of substances is abolished: a single one replaces them all: the whole world *can* be plasticized, and even life itself since, we are told, they are beginning to make plastic aortas. (99)

Taking a cue from this intervention, one may argue that since the invention of plastics, the Earth slips into a process of *(en)plasticization* that results in the "trans(g)local" and "transcorporeal" travelling of plastics through different earthly agents. Plastic happens to be a terrible invention which is characterized by pervasiveness, contamination, becoming, strangeness and an element of surprise. It is more of a medium than an embodiment because it is through plastics, humans and non-agencies can travel across the world. Take for example a "plastic bottle"–an anthropogenic product which can reach Polar Regions being guided by oceanic waves and flows. The reaching of a "plastic bottle" to Polar Regions can be interpreted in two ways: it is by exploiting "plastic bottles", human beings can make inroads into the distant territories which stand divested of 'human' presence for long; it triggers the process of *(en)plasticization* conditioned by the micropolitical engagement of a "plastic bottle" with the becoming of the earth. In short, the earth steps into a terrain of "plastic time" in the sense that the becoming of the earth has to comply with the becoming of the plastic thereby entailing *(en)plasticization* of ecology.

In *The Future of Hegel: Plasticity, Temporality and Dialectic*, Catherine Malabou has made attempts to re-contextualize Hegelian conception of "plasticity" by means of exploiting the etymological connotations of plastics. Malabou holds:

> . . . the concept of plasticity . . . in its first sense, describes or *designates the act of giving form* . . . the Greek *plassein* (πλσσειν), which means 'to model', 'to mould'. 'Plastic', as an adjective, means two things: on the one hand, to be 'susceptible to changes of form' or malleable (clay is a 'plastic' material); and on the other hand, 'having the power to bestow form, the power to mould'. . . . *Plasticité*, or 'plasticity', just like *Plaztizität* in German, describes the nature of that which is 'plastic', being at once capable of receiving and of giving form. (8)

Malabou perceptively reflects that the notion of plasticity is teasingly problematic because the ideas of "receiving and giving form" are conflated in it. One may take two examples to understand Malabou's critical conceptualization of plasticity. "Plastic material" is one such thing that describes the suppleness of the material and is also connotative of "multi-functionality" and "polymorphic" ability of the material. Put in other words, "plastic material" can assume any intended form and can get rid of any given algorithm. It suggests–that which is "plastic" in nature gets transformed in terms of both "intensive" and "extensive" becomings. Whereas "intensive" becoming of "plastic" allows it to get mixed up with different earthly matters through the process of "micro-plasticization", "extensive" becoming of the plastic ends up it forming "plastiglomerate". Malabou is also of this viewpoint that plasticity has both "formative" and "formable" power–which helps it transgress the pull of territorialization. Based on Malabou's understanding of "plasticity", one may contend that "plasticity" stands as a *raison d'art* for any sort of experimentation. Interestingly, the configuration of "plasticity" is steeped in precarity and fluidity. "Plasticity" works by the *logic of dissension* that might help one get over the problems of categorization. It also serves as a *governing logic* for transcending the limits of temporality.

Malabou has later on taken up the notion of plasticity in her latest works. For instance, she has come up with the notion of "destructive plasticity" in *Ontology of the Accident: An Essay on Destructive Plasticity*. It is argued that "plasticity" has to be "destructive" in nature in order to retain its "formative" and "formable" potentials: ". . . a plastic art of destruction. Yet destruction too is formative. A smashed up face is still a face, a stump a limb, a traumatized psyche remains a psyche. Destruction has its own sculpting tools" (4). She is pointing out that plasticity operates by the destruction of the self in the sense that it has to annihilate one "form" to move to another. In this regard, it needs to be mentioned that "plasticity" does not carry a pejorative connotation as such, rather it follows the principle of deconstruction. Transmutability of "plastic art" speaks of how "construction" and "destruction" get neutralized by "deconstruction" which attests to the "surprising potentials" of plastic. Later on, a number of critical thinkers have taken up plasticity in different contexts. For example, Ranjan Ghosh has elaborately explained "plasticity" in "Plastic Literature" which, according to him, can be ". . . our new poetics of generating literary capital and rethinking world literature" (277).

Figurations of plasticity are many in number and densely nuanced. In order to understand the polymorphous quality of plasticity, one can think of considering "rhizomatics" and "nomadism" as propounded by Gilles Deleuze and Felix Guattari in *A Thousand Plateaus*. According to Deleuze and Guattari, rhizome has six intrinsic principles–"connection", "heterogeneity", "multiplicity", "signifying rupture", "cartography" and "decalcomania". Just like a rhizome can "connect" and "disconnect" itself at its disposal, "plastic", too, has the potential to "connect" and "disconnect" itself from a number of forms. As "plastic" works by the tension between "connection" and "disconnection", it inherently possesses a sort of heterogeneity within itself, which leads it to dodge the snares of homogenization. For instance, there are innumerable kinds of 'plastic art' which exist by means of refusing codification. Interestingly, a "plastic figure" bears many shades in itself, which allows it to "receive and give" "forms" further. Plastic can get fit into different forms because of its transmutability. In other words, it is because of their inherent "multiplicity", plastics can get unfolded themselves. If one tries to mould plastic into different forms, he can figure it out as a "trace of a movement". Rhizomatic progression of plasticity through space and time is characterized by "points of escape", which vouches for its deterritorializing movements.

One may choose to find semblances between plasticity and nomadism in that just like a nomad, plasticity can hardly be realized in terms of fixity and rigidity. If one looks into the functionality of plasticity from the perspective of Nomadism, one may understand that plasticity does not comply with linearity and sequentiality of History. It is the very "suppleness" of plasticity that leads itself to the nomadic ways of "becoming-other". In other words, plasticity cannot be bound up by the threads of segmentarity, for the very "suppleness" of plasticity accounts for its inclination to the "lines of flight". Nomadic travel of plasticity bears the potential of bringing out radical alterations in our understanding of the world around us. It is also true that the nomadic quality of plasticity can help one both "deterritorialize" the regimented notion of ecology and add up newer dimensions to it.

It would be inappropriate to claim that ecology is a monolithic human construct which has been coined to categorize the world around us. One may first think of the etymological differences between "ecology" and "ecosophy":

whereas the former speaks for the scientific enquiry of the interconnections between organic and inorganic worlds, the latter is suggestive of a densely interdisciplinary framework required to intervene in the complex ecological problems. Generally speaking, ecology is referred to understand Nature which stands in contrast with another human construct called "culture". In *Being Ecological*, Timothy Morton reflects: "Thinking in an ecological way means letting go of this idea of nature–it sounds incredible, but that's only because we're so habituated to certain ways of accessing and executing and otherwise 'interpreting' things such as lakes, trees, cows, snow, sunshine, and wheat" (xxxiv). Morton is right in arguing that one has to do away with "Nature" to deterritorialize limited jurisdiction of ecology. It is undeniably true that the notion of ecology cannot remain restricted within Nature. The borders of ecology are extended to culture, economics, politics, religion, aesthetics, ethics, and so on. For instance, Guttarian's perception of "ecology" is three-fold: "environment", "social relation" and "human subjective". Guattari puts emphasis on ethico-political understanding of the world around us so that human developments can be made in harmony with that of the Earth. Ethico-political framework can also be helpful in drawing out a roadmap for the futurity of ecology. One may also be reminded of "A Thousand Ecologies", Ronald Bogue conspicuously pluralizes ecology in the following way: ". . . if thought may unfold across a thousand plateaus, there are a thousand ecologies that would unfold within those plateaus, a thousand ways of attempting to create a new collectivity and a new earth" (55). Taking a cue from Bogue's understanding, one may say that experimentation with "ecology" is quite possible and more importantly, it is required to open up the functional horizon of it.

It is true that limited functional space cannot allow ecology to address some emerging issues like the differential progression of the earth through human development. In the post-neoliberal era, the human world has advanced to a large extent in the fields of technology and commerce. Whereas, earlier, ecological threats included deforestation, illegal poaching, trafficking of expensive woods, and so on, nowadays, ecological threats incorporate mineralization of plastics into the earth, techno-commercial wastes, toxic debris of industries, climate change, soil erosion, and so on. This situation calls for experimentation with ecology.

At this critical juncture, the notion of "plasti(e)cological thinking" can be put forward. "Plasti(e)cological thinking" generally relates to both "plastic ecology" and an ecology that stands covered by plastics. "Plastic ecology" refers to the "plastic becoming" of ecology. Ecology cannot but be "plastic" in nature in order to be both transformative and transformable. An epistemic intervention into the pervasive presence of ecology suggests that it is because of the inherent plasticity, an ecology can run into a thousand other ecologies. Interactions between ecologies result in the "intensive" and "extensive" becomings of the ecologies involved. Plasticity also accounts for the constant alteration of ecology through time and space. "Plastic ecology" connotes that ecology can at once shape up the ontologies of its constitutive elements and at times can get transfigured by the same. The problematic issue regarding it is that "plastic ecology" can hardly be codified and territorialized. It is more of a matter of experience, for it follows the principles of rhizomatics.

Nowadays, plastics cover up the ecology around us so much that it does not let it function to its own tune. The intervention of plastics in the becoming of the Earth leaves a terrible impact on humanity at large in the sense that it puts the existence of natural species at risk and makes the Earth all the more inhabitable to all. It is as it were that plastics start to rule the Earth and impact several natural processes of the Earth. For example, one may think of how oceans stand covered up by plastics which get into the bodies of sea species, contaminate their bodies, and transform them into a veritable "plastiglomerate". Interestingly, the dominance of plastics on the earth forces the Earth to step into spheres of "plastic time" and "plastic memory". It means that when an entity of the earth gets dominated by plastics, it has to comply with the dissolving mechanism of plastics. Plastics do not have limited life span like human beings and thus can carry the memories of how it rules the roost. Unlike human memory, "plastic memory" is durable and supple in nature. "Plastic memory" can take up different forms but can hardly be erased. It is because of this quality, "plastic memory" directly questions the supremacy and authoritative position of the Earth's memory.

An understanding of "plasti(e)cological thinking" can lead the humanity to incorporate the massive role of non-human agency in transforming the Earth. "Plasti(e)cological" insights can help ecocritics to address how plastics, among other toxic and terrible pollutants, can transform the geohistory of the Earth; can result in the production of "plastiglomerate"; can take control of the supposedly independent operations of the Earth. It shall also open up how the sphere of ecology can be stretched off to non-human agencies. Stagnancy of ecology can be removed by means of considering "plasti(e)cological thinking" which underlines the "supple segmentarity" of ecology. Theoretical exploration of the "plasticity" of ecology can help one figure out the continuous formation, deformation and transformation of ecology through time and space. "Plasti(e)cological thinking" actually advances and upgrades ecology to such an extent that it can tackle contemporary threats at large. New variants of ecology would come up to enrich human understanding of ecology and would subsequently provide epistemic interstices.

The notion of "plasti(e)cological thinking" can productively be folded into the nuances of planetary thinking in that whereas planetary thinking exposes co-existential becomings of the constituents of the planet Earth, it seems to be capable of explaining how "plasti(e)cological thinking" can help one spell out networked interconnections among different ecologies on the planet. Planetary thinking can also lay down non-human dimensions of "plasti(e)cological thinking" which, unlike anthropocentric worldviews, brings out non-human ways of knowing the transformability of different planetary ecologies. Planetary thinking can also be held instrumental in revealing that "plasti(e)cological thinking" is not just only an alternative critical tool of enquiry to the hackneyed understanding of the planetary ecology as a stable and inflexible entity but also is a terrasophical method backed up by geophilosophical insights, which is capable of elucidating co-intensive and co-extensive becomings of the planet Earth.

In *Theory of the Earth*, Thomas Nail has cogently spoken about the processual dimensions of the Earth which by means of its free intensities stands in a state of "becoming". Nail pertinently reflects:

> The earth is a material process continuous with the expansion of the universe that produced, and continues to produce, the earth. The earth is not a vacuum-sealed object cut off from the outside. Nor is it an unchanging or uniformly changing substance following autonomous processes. Geology flows from cosmology . . . I lay out a kinetic theory of the earth that I call "geokinetics." Geokinetics has three aspects: the flow of matter, the fold of elements, and the circulation of planetary fields. . . . We cannot correctly understand the earth as a being because it is a becoming. Trying to determine the being of matter is a similarly flawed approach. Matter neither is nor is not, but flows, folds, and circulates. Matter is not a being but a becoming. (19-25)

Nail has laid down a theory of "geokinetics" which is grounded in the interplay among flow, fold and circulation. Following Nail's contention, one may argue that material fluidity in combination with the processes of enfoldment and circulation does not allow the Earth to stand in compliance with the forces of territorialization and consequently, accounts for its "becoming". This "becoming" of the planet Earth stands embedded in the complex networking between different planetary ecologies. Micropolitical engagements with the geokinetic becomings of the planet Earth can help one understand how the operative logic of Earth is consequent upon the continual transformation of interactions among planetary ecologies. As far as nuanced intersections and interactions among different planetary ecologies are concerned, one may tenably take recourse to "plasti(e)cological thinking" to figure out how transformation of one planetary ecology impacts its adjacent planetary ecologies and is impacted by the becomings of other planetary ecologies. In short, "trans(in)fusive" tendency of planetary ecology can well be understood with the help of "plasti(e)cological thinking" which can be useful in unfolding micropolitical interactions among different ecologies. Intensive transformation of each planetary ecology does not only condition the "becoming(s)" of other planetary ecologies but also it accounts for the "relations of exteriority" that is responsible in actualizing the physical alterations of different ecologies. Put it in other words, "plasti(e)cological thinking" is, in actuality, instrumental in pulling out a component from a planetary ecological assemblage and subsequently in plugging it into another planetary ecological assemblage thereby exposing how "relations of exteriority" play a pivotal role in conditioning (un)folding and (en)folding planetary ecological dimensions.

"Plasti(e)cological thinking" stands imbued in the "quanta of deterritorialization" and "supple segmentarity", which can help one figure out its innate "lines of flight". In other words, "plasti(e)cological thinking" relates flexibility, fluidity and fecundity, which are intricately embedded in the planetary ecological interactions. "Plasti(e)cological thinking" also sets out to dismantle and disrupt geopolitical territorialization of planetary ecologies and to lay bare how the symbiotic synthesis among the folds of the planet Earth stands up against rigid segmentations. Put in simple words, different types of planetary ecology stand too connected to be separated from each other and the sliding of one planetary ecology into the domain of another makes "Plasti(e)cological thinking" a timely necessity. "Plasti(e)cological thinking" always works towards liberating planetary ecologies which are often regressively mapped in terms of territories and strata. The innate dynamicity of the planet Earth in general and particularly "geokinesis" of the material entities of the planet Earth can be figured out with the help of "plasti(e)cological thinking" which at once shows the transformation of the non-human world and at times uncovers the plasticity of planetary ecology. Put in Deleuzo-Guattari fashion, "plasti(e)cological thinking" seeks to unleash planetary ecologies from the bounds of segmentarity which makes every planetary ecology stand cut off from other adjacent ones. As "plasti(e)cological thinking" is premised on the "quanta of deterritorialization", it encourages one to interrogate the processes of territorial rigidification, stratified consciousness of planetary ecology and binaristic formulations concerning human and non-human worlds. Rhizomatic in its configuration and differential in its operation and transgressive in its orientation, "plasti(e)cological thinking" seeks to (un)conceal ecological overlapping, nomadic flows and folds of planetarity, transversal presencing of non-human agency and the Earth as a "Body without Organs" (BwO) or a "Plane of Consistency".

Here, one may take a pause and think: does the notion of "elemental politics" have any role to play in actualizing "plasti(e)cological thinking"? In other words, does "plasti(e)cological thinking" help one delve deeper into its intensive micropolitics? Thinking with "saturation" might be effective in answering these questions and in order to do so, one may be reminded of "Thinking with Saturation beyond Water: Threshold, Phase Change and the Precipitate" where Melody Jue and Rafico Ruiz critically reflect: ". . . [to] think with saturation is to acknowledge the co-presence of multiple phenomena within the complexity of our symbiogenic world" (3). Jue and Ruiz mean to say that saturation thinking can potentially open up critical ways of getting engaged with "elemental politics" of the planetary Earth. According to Jue and Ruiz, saturation thinking is consequent upon the interplay among "Threshold", "Phase Change" and "the Precipitate" and thus ". . . Saturation is not only about elements in political configurations, but about the politics of elemental formation through their mediation" (4). Thinking with the elemental agency is potent enough to lay bare when an element reaches threshold position, it tends to go for a "phase change" and finally ends up in the "precipitate" state. It is true that elemental mediation stands characterized by relationality, intentionality and micropolitics. Jue and Ruiz further argue that they ". . . think of elementality not as a taxonomy of substances, but as a politics of co-presences under flux" (5). Following this contention, one may argue that saturation thinking actually ". . . opens a space for considering the interrelated agencies that inhere in a situation" (5). In a nutshell, saturation thinking which stands grounded in elemental politics can help one understand how one material agency develops in parallel with other counterparts and how the developments of the latter impact the growth of the former. It at once interrogates human-centred approaches to planetarity and at times encourages critical thinkers to engage themselves with the rhizomatic growth of planetary agencies. Jue and Ruiz have thus pertinently put forward:

> Saturation enables us to engage with phenomena as they concurrently emerge across specific locales and scales, necessitating an analytical sensitivity to multiple saturants. . . . Saturation is a call to build a radical

theory of milieu that holds aqueous, contextual relations up for analysis
(7).

Keeping the discursive paradigms of saturation thinking in mind, it can be argued that "plasti(e)cological thinking" can safely bank on elemental politics
that saturation thinking offers inasmuch as the "plasti(e)cological thinking"
framework is intended to examine the multiplicities of a give situation which
comprises intermixing and intermingling of human and non-human agencies.
"Plasti(e)cological thinking" is capable of (un)concealing micropolitical engagements between different material agencies which grow up by interacting
with each other. For example, one may imagine a coastal area which stands
fraught with plastics, human wastes and toxic non-human products–the presence of all these elements are vicious for the marine ecologies under the ocean.
Thrown-out plastics tend to slip into the process of micro-plasticization with
the existing minerals under the pedosphere and are then likely to contaminate
it further. Mixing of microplastics with the natural minerals of the Earth impacts the productivity of the pedosphere and when it gets engulfed by sea
waves, it is likely to get precipitated in the tangles of marine ecologies which
are ultimately affected and damaged. Rightly has Ranjan Ghosh argued in
"Plastic Literature" and in "The Plastic Controversy":

> Within a labour intensive, garbological, and fast-capitalist system, plas-
> tic continues to spread and is recycled, enhancing the complex
> networks of access and excess. The translocationality of plastic through
> plastic pervasiveness and scopious contamination represents a spatial
> consciousness where plastic seeps into salt, water, soil, animal and hu-
> man bodies, media, and our psychosis, mostly in non-linear, non-
> hierarchical, fragmentary mobility and fluidity. (278)
> Plastiglomerate, this new-found geo-reality, is a product of hardened
> molten plastic holding sediment, basaltic lava fragments, and organic
> debris, natural debris, and sedimentary grains. . . . As plastic is made to
> sieve through into the remotest non-human corners of this planet, the
> subterranean infiltration is no less emphatic – call it plastiturbation. . . .
> Plastifossilization" is a relentless and inexorable process that rechar-
> acterizes an already unstable earth that is a "compilation machine, an
> assembly line," where "trash, construction debris, coal ash, dredged
> sediments, petroleum contamination, green lawns, decomposing bod-
> ies, and rock ballast not only alter the formation of soil but themselves
> form soil bodies, and in this respect are taxonomically indistinguishable
> from soil." (no. pag.)

Ghosh consistently reflects on the trans(in)fusive[1] becomings of plastics through a number of material elements and it results in the geoerotic alterations of the planet Earth. "Non-linear, non-hierarchical, fragmentary mobility and fluidity" of plastics impact interactions among different ecologies. "Plasti(e)cological thinking" backed up by "elemental politics" can help one figure out how the aspects of micro-plasticization stand checkered with the nuances of other planetary ecologies thereby calling for an inclusive and intensive, micropolitical and deterritorial engagement with the fluid co-extentialities of different planetary agencies.

Following the principles of "saturation thinking" in mind, one may argue that "plasti(e)cological thinking" calls for a symbiotic framework by means of which planetary events, planetary agential interactions and planetary health, among others, can well be examined. In actuality, "plasti(e)cological thinking" leads one to delve deeper into the simultaneous developments of different life forms and these life forms are in dialogue with each other. It aims at bringing out how life in its abstraction, that is, "zoe" travels through the "Plane of Consistency" and connects and disconnects human and non-human worlds at its disposal. Differential and heterogeneous growth of "zoe" while undergoing planetary ecologies can be figured out in terms of "plasti(e)cological thinking" in that epistemological framework of "plasti(e)cological thinking" is contingent upon "smooth politics"[2]. Stratigraphical inroads into the mediatedness existing between planetary ecologies can also be helpful in understanding how different planes like geological, geographical, cultural, political, economical and ecological, among others, interact with each other seamlessly. Thus, within the broad biosphere, there come geosphere, ecosphere and atmosphere. In fact, the limit of each sphere happens to be the convergence of two or more spheres.[3] Therefore, if one steps into the biosphere of the planet Earth, he is to be carried away by the limits of other converging spheres. At this point, one may reminded of Derrida's formulation of "limitrophy" which investigates ". . . what sprouts or grows at the limit, around the limit, by maintaining the limit, but also what feeds the limit, generates it, raises it, and complicates it" (29). Following Derridean formulation, one may reflect that limits existing between different spheres are "zones of indiscernibility"[4] inasmuch as limits are actually in kinesis. Kinetic dimensions of limits can be explored by "plasti(e)cological thinking" in that it encourages critical thinkers to look up to the intensive micropolitics which accounts for the deterritorial becomings of planetary ecologies. As different spheres are weaved together in a seamless chain of intermediation, there is the need for "plasti(e)cological thinking" which equips one to comprehend how in a given situation, a planetary event or a figuration of planetary illness stands at the crossroads of different intersecting planetary ecologies.

Brad Evans and Julian Reid happen to be two important critical thinkers who cogently argue in *Resilient Life: The Art of Living Dangerously* that "atmosis" could be held as an epistemological framework to understand the densely interconnected dimensions between different spheres:

> So how may we think the atmospheric-aesthetic-affective register differently? . . . however, can it begin without an appreciation of atmospheric transformation whose metamorphosis between recombinant elements is philosophically and scientifically accepted to be the source of new creations and worlds to come (136-137).

Evans and Reid are of the viewpoint that "atmosis" is productive of a "new" combination of elements which stand tied to each other by the logic of osmosis. Bio-Geo-Eco-At(os)mosis in particular refers to the way in which one sphere having low concentration sips into another sphere having high concentration through porous and fluid limits. Osmotic interactions between spheres are suggestive of the way different planetary ecologies having disparate concentration levels interact and intersect with each other. "Plasti(e)cological thinking" here comes in handy in explaining how one sphere stands folded into another one thereby forming a "Plane of Consistency". And the folding of one sphere into another entails a seamless and symbiotic whole which is charged up with the quanta of deterritorialization and destratification. It also lays bare how flows and folds of different spheres stand wedded to the ethics of desiring-production in that the nomadic infrastructure of planetary ecology resists itself from being caught up in the anthropocentric overtures. In short, "plasti(e)cological thinking" is able to lay down the distinctive resilience of planetary ecology, which, despite being subjected to exploitative human oeuvres, is guided by its self-sustaining healing mechanism.

"Plasti(e)cological thinking" could be held as an experiment in Ecopoetics in that on the one hand it allows one to examine the co-presences of different planetary elements under flux and on the other hand, it leads one to get engaged with the production of the new epistemological frameworks to map the becomings of planetary ecology. What is interesting about "plasti(e)cological thinking" is that it does not steer one to make critical inroads into a narrative with certain predispositions and presuppositions; rather, it allows one to fashion and refashion different factors associated with the notion of planetarity in new combinations, thereby intending to come up with suitable ecopoetical frameworks. Epistemic configuration of "plasti(e)cological thinking" does reflect aesthetic connotations which are worth considering while examining the representations of contemporary planetary concerns in different literary and cultural narratives. One of the important advantages of having "plasti(e)cological thinking" in the critical discourses is that it facilitates one to make transversal inroads into the massively mediated planetary ecologies. Therefore, "plasti(e)cological thinking" is a way forward in the era of New Materialism, Posthumanism[5] and Postanthropocentrism.

Notes

1. In *Trans(in)fusion: Reflections for Critical Thinking*, Ranjan Ghosh explains "trans(in)fusion" in the following words:

> Trans(in)fusion is a method of 'doing' and 'living' and our non method too – a map with which we begin to think through issues, disciplines, and discourses and expire at a point where the initial map remains with a smudge, a torn, frayed end, a splotch and, also, a few more maps that we could not help collecting down the way, we needed on our journey, we indulged procuring to effect a more exciting finish. . . . Trans(in)fusion, for me, is less a compulsion and more a campaign. It is an experience that we, most often, cannot do without – a delectation, an allurement, a latency and education. (2)

2. In "Smooth Politics", Malcolm Bull reflects: ". . . although a smooth politics may be unconstrained by preexisting social forms, it is, for that reason constrained in the social forms that it can take" (226). Bull calls for smooth politics which are guided by the forces of deterritorialization can replace "striated politics" that is often employed to split up the Earth into territories and strata.

3. In "Kinopolitics: Borders in Motion", Thomas Nail cogently puts forward:

> Kinopolitics is the theory and analysis of social motion: the politics of movement. Instead of analysing societies as primarily static, spatial or temporal, kinopolitics or social kinetics understands them primarily as 'regimes of motion'. Societies are always in motion: directing people and objects, reproducing their social conditions (periodicity), and striving to expand their territorial, political, juridical and economic power through diverse forms of expulsion. In this sense, it is possible to identify something like a political theory of movement. (190)

Nail actually refers to the fact that "borders are in constant motion and have a material non-human political agency of their own . . . the primary function of borders is to keep people out or let them in . . . the main function of the border is not to stop movement but to circulate it." (194).

4. In *What is Philosophy?*, Deleuze and Guattari reflect:

> Territory and earth are two components with two zones of indiscernibility–deterritorialization (from territory to the earth) and reterritorialization (from earth to territory). (86)

5. In "Posthuman Systems", Simone Bignall and Rosi Braidotti attempt to map the salient strands of 'posthuman turn' in the following words:

The 'posthuman turn'–defined as the convergence of posthumanism with post-anthropocentrism–is a complex and multidirectional discursive and material event. It encourages us to build on the generative potential of the critiques of humanism developed by radical epistemologies that aim at a more inclusive practice of becoming-human. . . . Deleuze's geo-zoe-ethological philosophy, resting on the vital materialism he draws from revisiting Spinoza, Nietzsche and Bergson, is particularly useful in stressing that we should abandon hierarchical comparisons in deciding the value or operative potential of humanity or a plant or a fly (for example), since these life-forms inhabit, or comprise, mutually affective 'inter-kingdoms'. (1)

Works Cited

Barthes, Roland. *Mythologies.* The Noonday Press, 1957.

Bhandar, Brenna, and Jonathan Goldberg-Hiller. "Introduction: Staging Encounters." In *Plastic Materialities: Politics, Legality and Metamorphosis in the Work of Catherine* Malabou, edited by Bhandar and Goldberg-Hiller, Duke University Press, 2015, pp. 1-33.

Bignall, Simone, and Rosi Braidotti. "Posthuman Systems." *Posthuman Ecologies Complexity and Process after Deleuze*, edited by Braidotti and Bignall, Rowman and Littlefield, 2019, pp. 1-16.

Bogue, Ronald. "A Thousand Ecologies." In *Deleuze/Guattari & Ecology*, edited by Bernd Herzogenrath, Palgrave Macmillan, 2009, pp. 42-56.

Brydson, J.A. *Plastic Materials.* Butterworth-Heinemann, 1999.

Bull, Malcolm. "Smooth Politics." *Empire's New Clothes Reading Hardt and Negri*, edited by Paul A. Passavant and Jodi Dean, Routledge, 2004, pp. 220-233.

Deleuze, Gilles, and Felix Guattari. *A Thousand Plateaus: Capitalism and Schizophrenia.* University of Minnesota Press, 1987.

–. *What is Philosophy?* Columbia University Press, 1994.

Derrida, Jacques. *The Animal That Therefore I Am.* Edited by Marie-Luise Mallet, Fordham rUniversity Press, 2008.

Evans, Brad, and Julian Reid. *Resilient Life: The Art of Living Dangerously.* Polity Press, 2014.

Ghosh, Ranjan. "Plastic Literature." *University of Toronto Quarterly*, vol. 88, no. 2, 2019, pp. 277-291. https://muse.jhu.edu/article/732562.

–. "The Plastic Controversy." *Critical Inquiry*, Feb. 4, 2021. https://critinq. wordpress.com/2021/02/04/the-plastic-controversy/.

–. *Trans(in)fusion: Reflections for Critical Thinking.* Routledge, 2021.

Jue, Melody, and Rafico Ruiz, editors. *Saturation: An Elemental Politics.* Duke University Press, 2021.

Malabou, Catherine. *Ontology of the Accident: An Essay on Destructive Plasticity.* Translated by Carolyn Shread, Polity Press, 2012.

–. *The Future of Hegel: Plasticity, Temporality and Dialectic.* Translated by Lisabeth During, Routledge, 2005.

Morton, Timothy. *Being Ecological.* MIT Press, 2018.

Nail, Thomas. *Theory of the Earth.* Stanford University Press, 2021.

–. "Kinopolitics: Borders in Motion." *Posthuman Ecologies Complexity and Process after Deleuze*, edited by Rosi Braidotti and Simone Bignall, Rowman and Littlefield, 2019, pp. 183-204.

Plamondon, Chantal, and Jay Sinha. *Life Without Plastic: The Practical Step-by-Step Guide to Avoiding Plastic to Keep Your Family and the Planet Healthy.* Page Street Publishing, 2017.

Chapter 3

Contextualizing *Plasti(e)cological Thinking*: Reading Select Indian Eco-texts

This chapter aims at providing an in-depth contextualization of different epistemological strands of "plasti(e)cological thinking" with particular references to Sudeep Sen's *EroText: desire, disease, delusion, dream,* downpour, and *Anthropocene: Climate Change, Contagion, Consolation,* and Sumana Roy's *How I Became a Tree.* In doing so, it also seeks to put forward that subsumption of "plasti(e)cological thinking" to the domain of critical thinking seems to be capable of leading one to get past stratified planetary thinking paradigms and thereby opening up new avenues of symbiotic thinking models which acknowledge co-presences and co-becomings of planetary entities. In this chapter, readers are shown how to select Indian eco-texts corroborate the operativity of "plasti(e)cological thinking" which, being grounded in the epistemological intersections among New Materialism, Posthumanism and Postanthropocentrism, can put the spotlight on the "points of departure" or what Deleuze and Guattari call in *A Thousand Plateaus* "lines of rupture" or "lines of flight", which account for the co-intensive and co-extensive becomings of planetary "elemental politics" embodied by earthly entities. In this regard, it needs to be clearly mentioned that select Indian eco-texts are specifically picked up, for these are found to be fittingly capable of bolstering epistemological configurations of "plasti(e)cological thinking" elucidated in great detail in the previous chapter.

Sudeep Sen's *EroText: desire, disease, delusion, dream, downpour* (2019; originally published in 2016 by Random House India)

Sudeep Sen (1964–) happens to be one of the contemporary Indian poets who has carved out a singular niche in the gamut of Contemporary Indian Poetry in English by producing a number of remarkable poetic anthologies including *Postmarked India: New Selected Poems, Rain, Aria, Fractals: New and Selected Poems, EroText, Blue Nude: New Poems and Ekphrasis,* and *Anthropocene: Climate Change, Contagion, Consolation.* Fashioned in the garb of micro-fiction, *EroText* is divided into five sections and each section takes up different themes pertaining to the subtle of *EroText*. Interestingly, each micro-fictional account of *EroText* is soaked in brevity, precision, unconventionality and micro-fluidity of emotion. *EroText* takes into account a wide range of planetary ecology starting from the (trans/inter)corporeal connectivity of the planet Earth up to the phenomenon of downpour that cuts across bio-geo-eco-spheres.

In "Magnetizing Dead Bones", the speaker poetically depicts an artificially programmed 'dead body' on a computer screen and subtly engages readers with the usual proceedings of a post–mortem. Ensconced in between "life" and "death", the speaker unfolds a spooky conversation between the person who does post-mortem and the "dead body" (supposedly the speaker himself) whose digital image is projected on the screen with the help of artificial technology:

> The person in the room can sense the
> electricity, invisible photons lighting
> up this intimately controlled space. The
> transfer of magnetism between us, with
> its latent live power, would be dangerous
> at this stage–both of us know that.
> . . .
> My body now has a hollow feeling
> running through it as if all the bones
> have been stripped out, leaving only
> the intangible flesh to find its shape. As
> long as I am harnessed to the electrodes,
> connected to its current, the shape will
> be retained artificially to deceive the
> onlooker. As long as there is no power
> failure, I can present myself amicably. (*EroText* 33-35)

This spooky interaction between a living body and an artificially programmed body can be interpreted with the help of "plasti(e)cological thinking" in that it is the transversal trajectory of "zoe" which at once connects two different "life-forms" and at times lays out the sliding of the human world into the digital world and the other way round. "Plasti(e)cological thinking" seems to be able to explain how human and non-human (including trans-human) ecologies stand in constant dialogue with each other. It also lays out transcorporeal intersections between living and dead bodies–a phenomenon which reminds one of the dialectical interplay between fluidity and fixity, placidity and excitability. It needs to be made clear that the spooky interactions between the two kinds of body are charged up with suppleness and flexibility, changeability and non-conformity. Therefore, when the two disparate corporeal ecologies are made to interact, these tend to get (en)folded into a multiplicity.

In "Wishbones, Arias, Memories", the speaker reflects on the intra-corporeal ecologies: "My heart still sends just enough oxygen/ to duel the think tank. It stays artificially/ active, in fact overactive, enough for/ a normal person to be electrocuted" (*EroText* 36). It suggests that the speaker "feel trapped" (*EroText* 38) in his own body and thus, imaginatively looks up for:

> . . . bones, not bones
> from the dead, but plastic ones, ones that
> allow a child to learn the building blocks
> of life, to construct and set up a model
> for their life, to feel the tactility of life
> itself. (*EroText* 39)

Here, the speaker clearly articulates why he prefers "plastic ones" to the "bones from the dead" and this poetic expression stands soaked in Malabou's notion of plasticity. "Plasti(e)cological thinking" here comes in handy for one who is interested in delving deeper into the miraculous potentials of plastics in receiving and giving "forms" at one's disposal. It also facilitates one in understanding the transformative and transformational potentials of plastics in constructing and reconstructing models for life to be learned by children. "Plasti(e)cological thinking" also stands capable of unpacking how a "plastic" model helps one in figuring out "the tactility of life" itself.

In "Fever Pitch", the speaker engages readers with the miraculous process of childbirth, which requires the collective operation of a number of bodily organs. The bodily assemblage of "zoe", chemicals and spatial externality with(in) a test tube strikes the wonder of the speaker:

> The seductiveness of a slim tall
> transparent glass tube–the
> curved silver juices it contains–
> is such that it makes me forget the news
> of the birth of a new child. Human
> life and inert chemical life compete in
> insidious ways, the same way fact and
> fiction do, as do desire ad disgust,
> illness and passion. (*EroText* 42)

"Plasti(e)cological thinking" through this poetic expression connotes that the act of giving birth to a child is a matter of deterritorial multiplicity which is contingent upon the "lines of rupture". Bodily formation of "life" through the intersections among several associate factors reminds one of how the physical exteriority of the planet Earth slips into the differential becomings of "life" through corporeality. "Plasti(e)cological thinking" helps one mark co-presences of different factors under flux and the micropolitics of the womb as well: "At the point of birth,/there is the dearth of the womb itself, but/ one lives–so there may be hope." (*EroText* 46). Following "plasti(e)cological thinking", one may argue that the womb has micropolitics of its own, which lets it get exhausted at the expense of producing a baby. So, the subtle interplay between life and death, micropolitics of the womb and AI aided scientific advancements in the field of gynecology can be mapped by the help of "plasti(e)cological thinking" which lays bare how transcorporeal differentiality stands at the crossroads of different ecologies–medical, biological, political, cultural, and philosophical.

Whereas in "Heavy Water", the speaker draws a connection between water and pain to underscore how "intensity" transversally cuts across "water" and "pain" thereby pointing at their nomadic singularities:

> There is something deeply arthritic
> about water and pain, the way
> water seeps into unexpected
> fissures in bones, the way it conducts
> pain itself–operationally, electrically.
> . . .
> Intensity
> Is a peculiar thing–its measurements
> are tactile and ephemeral, quantifiable
> and infinite. It is measurable, its heat
> and depth fathomable.
> . . .
> But heavy heart, like heavy water, is
> difficult to dissolve–their melting and
> boiling points register unusual scales–
> scales that peal and peel. Echo and layer,
> untying each and every fibre that breath
> requires in order to survive. (*EroText*, 48-51)

The speaker here interestingly suggests that although water has its palliative potential in tempering the "intensity" of pain, it augments pain significantly when it seeps into "fissures in bones". The fluidity of water interacts with the heaviness of pain when it comes to the poignancy of a human heart. "Plasti(e)cological" insights lead one to think how the micropolitical interactions between water and pain at the level of "intensity" get exteriorized "heavy heart" that is difficult to calm down. A human body is made of a watery component which does not always stand squared with 'pain' that is inflected into the body externally. So, the human heart happens to be a fertile site for the meeting of "watery element" and "pain"–although the melting and boiling points of both water and pain differ in degrees. Sen has drawn another image of ecological trans(in)fusion in "'O' Zone" which relates how a patient complaining of serious breathing difficulties and respiratory malfunction is provided emergency medical support while he is battling against death:

> My face–confined in the transparency
> of plastic, frosted glass and thin air–
> regains for a moment the normalcy of
> breathing. It is a brief magical world.
> The oxygen in my blood is in short
> supply. I feel each and every electron's
> charge, spurring my senses.
> . . .
> My breathing is temporarily back
> now–electrolysed, perfectly pitched
> and nebulized–as narrow transparent
> tubes feed dreams into my wide opaque
> palate. (*EroText* 52-53)

It is the plastic mask that seals off his face from the external world and sets the ambience ready for putting the ailing body on an artificial support system. It is a prerequisite for supplying oxygen to a patient as it serves both to disconnect the ailing body from the physical ecology of the Earth and to connect it to a "magical world" which helps him survive for the time being. "Plasti(e)cological thinking" informs one how plastics play an instrumental role in reaffirming "life" to the patient by means of sustaining the oxygen supply in the body. When the patient feels slightly "back now", he can figure out how the plastic mask has been tirelessly working to help him feel "electrolysed, perfectly pitched and nebulized". It means that the bodily ecology of the ailing patient gets life-saving sustenance, that is, oxygen, from the external ecology through the plastic mask and thus regains energy from with(in). It also suggests that plastic mask does not only connect two disparate ecologies but forges a Body

without Organs (BwO) as it were in that it at once erases bodily boundaries between the human body and AI, and at times seeks to recognize seamless
interactions between diverse ecologies– "narrow transparent/ tubes feed
dreams into my wide opaque/ palate". One may now refer to Sen's other poem
named "Desire" which reflects an image of intercourse which is supposed to
get ended up in a sexual union:

> You–lying inverted like the letter
> 'c'–arch yourself deliberately, wanting
> the warm press of my lips, their wet to
> coat the skin that is bristling, burning,
> breaking into sweats of desire–sweet
> juices of imagination. (*EroText*; 92)

This example underlines how two disparate bodies are getting up for a deterritorialized assemblage which entails seamless interactions between the human
body and the physical world. In short, the "desiring-production" of the body
gets actualized when sexual union takes place. Dismantling of ecological bar-
riers among planetary elements is done through the productive potentials of
"desire" which opens up a "Plane of Consistency" for the lovers. And
"plasti(e)cological thinking" can help one map the rhizomatic progression of
"desire" that holds two disparate corporeal ecologies together on the "Plane of
Consistency". This contention can be consolidated by referring to "Absences"
which draws on global oceanic connectivity, bodies and desire to underline
how these "elements" work together in the erasure of strata and territories
which render the Earth a territorialized geo-spatiality:

> I imagine the wet breaking the anchor
> loose, defying gravity, current and
> electricity, as photons propel and burn
> even the wild salted expanse into a
> monument, a desire, permanent like
> the ocean bed, its pulses uncontrollably
> rocking–the waters, the bodies, the
> dreams. (*EroText* 94)

This poetic excerpt seeks to map the strands of "absence" in terms of "desiring-
production" which streamlines "the waters, the bodies, the dreams" thereby
pointing at the intensive plasticity of planetary ecology. In addition to it, Sen

has attempted to explore the micropoetics[1] of "desire" in "Taste" which succinctly captures the supple segmentarity of desire in the following words:

> The taste of
> desire is the taste of its warm lingering
> aftertaste. (*EroText* 95)

It reminds one of how "plasti(e)cological thinking" celebrates the becoming of an ecological phenomenon through banking on "elemental politics" which is contingent upon "the threshold, phase change and the precipitate". In "Silence", the speaker lays down "plastic" potentials of "desire" in transforming "silence" into "words":

> Desire melting even
> silence to words–word's colour bleed
> incarnate, as your lips whisper softly
> the secrets of your silence. (*EroText* 108)

"Plasti(e)cological thinking" may lead one to argue that in the sphere of ecological continuum, "desire" undergoes "elemental politics" and turns "silence" into "words" which bespeak "pure white silence" (*EroText* 108). It means that neither "silence" stands aloof from "words" nor "words" stay indifferent bleeding incarnate. It is the "desire" that eliminates differences between silence and words, words and colour, colour and meaning, meaning and silence.

One may drag another poetic instance to corroborate the viability of "plasti(e)cological thinking" in advancing the domain of planetary thinking. In "Knowledge, Need", the speaker philosophically remarks:

> The more you know, the less
> you need'–but that is not
> true at all for thirst, water,
> or rain. (*EroText*, 228)

Here, the speaker tries to forge a world which does not conform to the common dictum but follows its own operative logic that stands wedded to the three strands of kinesis, that is, flow, fold and circulation. Whereas the word "thirst" refers to the living organisms, "water" metaphorically implies water bodies that stand grounded in the Earth and "rain" is suggestive of bio-geo-eco-atmospheric linkage that H_2O renders. Streamlining "thirst", "water" and "rain" entails erasure of strata and territories, and subsequently formation of a deterritorialized assemblage that knows no limits. Following the tenets of "plasti(e)cological thinking", one may tenably argue that nuanced intersections among human, non-human and ahuman worlds as reflected in the poems incorporated in *EroText* need to be examined to figure out the differential progression of planetarity that stands in conformity with layered interactions between ecologies.

Anthropocene: Climate Change, Contagion, Consolation (2021)

Sudeep Sen has recently come up with another excellent poetic anthology named *Anthropocene* which is an amalgamation of some old poems along with many new poems pertaining to climate change, contagion and consolation. The title of the poetic anthology is suggestive of that the included poems seem to reflect on how human beings engage themselves in various activities to shape and reshape Anthropocene while particularly responding to climate change in particular. Climate change happens to be one of the biggest threats that Anthropocene nowadays confronts in spite of being the superior species on the Earth. Etiology of climate change followed by its resultant alterations in the lives of human and non-human beings are poetically explored by Sen to make readers aware of the way the Earth responds to the human-led exploitations. Although Sen primarily attempts to figure out Anthropocene in terms of climate change and its consequences, he also draws references to the pitfalls of Anthropocene, which need to be reformed to safeguard the Earth for the futurity and to redefine planetarity anew.

The book cover of Sen's *Anthropocene* does not merely consist of three yellow, pale and dissimilar leaves but the image of three leaves symbolically suggests the dire and dreadful impacts of contagion, infection and climate change. This image is also evocative of how dried up and yellow leaves look severely affected and infected by some unknown pests, which entails peripheral decay of the leaves. This is quite alarming for the Anthropocene referring to the human world which is quite indifferent to the way the natural world suffers the consequences of climate change. Discoloured, distorted and dissimilar image of the three leaves actually sets the tone of the book which unpacks how interactions between ecologies are affected by climate change. In "i.e. [that is]", the speaker, in the fashion of a dramatic monologue, vindicates why the sea has fallen silent over the years:

> i.e.
> because you hear–
> the sound

of a lone rustling leaf–
you hear the sea.
i.e.
because I consider
the sea silent–
you hear its silence
in my studio
i.e.
because of that–
the silence will not empty
the sea
of its leaves. (*Anthropocene*, 27)

Following "plasti(e)cological thinking", this silence of the sea can be interpreted in this way that sound and silence stand coalesced in the sea which
symbolically articulates the inexplicable sufferings of yellow and pest-infected
leaves by privileging silence over sound. It means that marine ecologies stand
someway connected to the miseries of infected leaves which fall back on the
agency of the sea to voice its plight as it were. Fluid connectivity existing between different ecologies is brilliantly explored by Sen in "Disembodied" which
reflects:

My lungs fuelled by Delhi's insidious toxic air
        echo asthmatic sounds, a new vinyl dub-remix.
Out universe–where radiation germinates from human follies,
        where contamination persists from mistrust,
        where pleasures of sex are merely a sport–
where everything is ambition,
everything is desire,   everything is nothing.
            Nothing and everything.   (*Anthropocene* 28)

This poetic expression reminds one of how the air quality in Delhi in recent
times has gone worse, which causes different kinds of respiratory disorders
leading to the proliferation of respiratory cancer cases.[2] Inordinate emission of
injurious gases from different industries accompanied by radiations of different sorts make the air quality extremely poor for the inhabitants of Delhi. What
is seriously alarming is that releasing of untreated gases not just only renders
the physical ecology of Delhi inhabitable for both flora and fauna, but it directly
impacts the speaker's lungs "insidiously", resulting in the production of "asth-
matic sounds" which is a clear indication of the fact that respiratory

malfunction has cut in his lungs. The corporeal ecology of the speaker cannot withstand the strikes of air pollution– insidious impacts of which subtly slip into different ecological frameworks. The speaker honestly agrees with the fact that radiation results from "human" follies thereby indicating how human beings stand responsible for causing disruptions to the planetary ecologies interactions. The issue of harmful radiation gets accompanied by the problem of contamination which is the outcome of "mistrust" that in actuality turns "the pleasures of sex" into a "sport". It is by equating "everything" to "desire", the speaker means to suggest that "everything" comes out of "nothing" as "nothing" and "everything" shares a hairline difference between themselves. "Plasti(e)cological thinking" may lead one to ponder over the fact that just as everything and nothing co-exist in a given situation, "desire" and "production of the new" go hand in hand. In other words, the interplay between the embodiment and disembodiment of air pollution can be overcome by tapping on the productive potentials of desire which is capable of turning the present condition of Delhi into a better place for living by means of dismantling, destratifying and deterritorializing the notion of ecological thinking. Sen thus rightly proclaims:

> White light everywhere,
>   but no one can recognize its hue,
> no one knows that there is colour in it–   all possible colours. (*Anthropocene* 28)

It is wisely suggested that "white" light is inclusive of all colours thereby suggesting how "white ecology" that stands aloof from human attention and examination, is capable of erasing fissures and fractures, ruptures and strictures–by means of which inclusivity of the planetary ecology is time and again denied. Here, one may be reminded of "White Ecology" where Bernd Herzogenrath spells out the onto-epistemological strands of 'white ecology':

> . . . a white ecology might provide a context in which different ecologies (different ecological fields, such as human, viral, chemical, etc., that all follow their own logics and trajectories) resonate with each other. An ecology motivated by the philosophy of Gilles Deleuze and Felix Guattari, I argue, can provide such a space–it is basically a call to think complexity, and to complex thinking, a way to think the environment as a negotiation of dynamic arrangements of cultural and natural forces, of both non-human and human stressors and tensors, both of which are informed and "intelligent." (1)

The notion of "white ecology" pertains to "plasti(e)cological thinking" in that like tatter, the former calls for a kind of thinking which takes into account complex and nuanced "negotiation of dynamic arrangements of cultural and natural forces". Sen rightly observes:

> Ice-caps are rapidly melting–too fast to arrest glacial slide.
> In the near future– there will be no water left
> or too much water that is undrinkable,
>   excess water that will drown us all.
> Disembodied floats. . . . (*Anthropocene* 29)

The speaker here is particular about how global warming accelerates the melting of "ice-caps", which results in the endangerment of humanity on the planet. Although the melting of "ice-caps" seems to be vicious to those who live in the polar regions and under the water, it is even more dangerous and appalling for the Anthropocene which hardly cares for the health of the planet. Maintenance of good planetary health is of utmost importance not just only to save the great source of drinking water but also to cordon off Anthropocene from the strikes of global warming, climate change and all other planetary ecological hazards. Here comes the significance of "plasti(e)cological thinking" that can lead one to explore some ways through which intensive and extensive becomings of the Earth can be understood comprehensively. Both the sufferings of human beings and the miseries of non-human worlds need to be taken together to look into how deteriorating conditions of planetary health impact transcorporeal interactions between ecologies.

In another poem titled "Global Warming", Sen takes up how global warming in particular puts the Anthropocene at risk and explicitly underlines the importance of "plasti(e)cological thinking" in redressing fractures and fissures in stratified planetary thinking:

> Climate patterns total disarray– defiantly altered
>   weather systems   topsy-turvy–
> global warming's   man-made havoc.
>   Earthquakes – overground, underground,
> undersea–
>   destruction, death,   cyclone, flood,
>   pestilence, pollution.
> Stillness, ever stiller still –   all still-born. (*Anthropocene* 30)

The speaker here clearly accuses human beings to have caused "global warm-ing" but interestingly, the aftermath of "global warming" does not stand confined in the ecology of the human world but seeks to transgress the limits of the human world and impact bio-geo-eco-atmospheres together. Global warming has not just only wrecked havoc on climate patterns on the planet but also results in "earthquakes". Significantly, the destructive figuration of "global warming" is not restricted to an "earthquake" but tends to assume different fluid and dynamic forms like "cyclone", "flood", "pollution" and so on. There-fore, "plasti(e)cological thinking" has to be put into practice to figure out transgressivity, spatio-temporality and affect(ability) of climate change across the "Plane of Consistency" that planetary ecology embodies. Although "global warming" seems to have led densely mediated planetary ecology to a standstill situation, free singularities of planetary ecology can be brought out to under-score its enormous potential to get past of fixity, stasis and rigid segmentarity. Following the poetic trail of "Global Warming", Sen, in "Rising Sea levels", draws the attention of readers to the rise of sea levels which, an offshoot of in-tense "global warming", ends up engulfing the surroundings of the lighthouse near the sea and in making it a "reality" for children and "a submerged memory" for the adults (*Anthropocene*; 31). It attests to the fact that "global warming" does not only affect marine ecologies alone, it alters the topograph-ical scenario near the lighthouse thereby suggesting that coastal ecology, too, stands extremely vulnerable and susceptible to the onslaughts of "global warming". Therefore, "plasti(e)cological thinking" seems to play an instru-mental role in guiding one through the densely mediated planetary ecology by means of exposing seamless and transcorporeal connectivity across the "Plane of Consistency".

Sen has attempted to map the consequences of "climate change" which does not only end up in the form of "global warming" but also entails unprecedented results. For example, in "Climate Change 2. Today", Sen reflects:

> Today there is
>   unexpected rain here–
> unseasonal snow
> . . .
> Dogs are coiled
>   Around each other,
> Birds' features
> Puffed up for warmth
>   Squirrels gone
> Back into hiding–

as we stare starkly
　　at the climate change
we've helped create. (*Anthropocene* 33)

This poetic excerpt clearly reflects that "unexpected rain" followed by "unseasonal snow" is the outcome of climate change which impacts planetary ecology in such a way that it alters natural seasonal cycles. Unexpected rain or unseasonal snowing does not only speak of the strange behaviour of the physical ecology of the Earth but also reveals how these events leave the human world in utter anxiety. It once again shows how climate change transgresses territorial limits and impacts the planetary ecology as a whole. "Plasti(e)cological thinking" here helps one understand how the non-human world gets equally affected by the pervasive and diffusive trajectories of climate change. It happens so because neither human ecology nor non-human ecology stands aloof from each other and thus, both kinds of ecology bear the brunt of being an integral part of transcorporeality. The speaker, although accuses the human world of having triggered climate change by doing a number of eco-unfriendly activities, considers "climate change" to have produced a sort of "terrible beauty" in "Climate Change 2":

climate change: changes
the terrible beauty of
　　unbearable heat. (*Anthropocene* 34)

It attests to the fact that climate change has at once exposed the vulnerability of the human world which considers itself superior to the rest of the world and at times has forced the "human world" to think with the notion of planetarity while responding to the "unbearable heat" of climate change.

　　"Plasti(e)cological thinking" bespeaks how one ecology stands folded into another one which stands striated by a number of ecologies thereby forming a sort of "rhizosphere" where it is difficult to trace the beginning or enduing except "the middle":

Something still remains–
Otherwise from ashes, smoke
Would not rise again (*Anthropocene* 152)

The fact of rising smoke from the ashes is suggestive of the plasticity of ecology which has been in a state of becoming. It is because of having quanta of deterritorialization, smoke "rises again" from the smoke. The emancipatory tendency of smoke is indicative of "co-intensive" and "co-existential" becomings of all the elements on the planet Earth.

Sumana Roy's *How I Became a Tree* (2017)

Sumana Roy happens to be an Indian writer who has penned down a number of literary works including *How I Became a Tree*, a non-fiction which is an ingenious mixing of memoir, literary history, botanical studies, philosophy of natural studies, and so on. Put under the grab of non-fiction, Roy subtly brings out how human, non-human and posthuman worlds stand enfolded into each other thereby forming a "Plane of Consistency". This book is replete with a number of references to "treelogy" and it offers some epistemological frameworks backed up by the strands of "plant humanities" so as to facilitate readers to grasp planetary ecological plasticity. Written in prose, Roy takes up planetary ecological concerns like the pitfalls of anthropocentrism, stratified philosophical approaches to the rigid singularity of ecology, and so on, by means of thrashing out the necessity of doing "plant humanities", and she also seeks to establish the nuanced interactions between human world and plant world. Here, one may stop and think: can "plasti(e)cological thinking" be extended to the study of non-fiction? This important question can be answered in this way that as long as "plasti(e)cological thinking" pertains to the advancement of planetary thinking, it can safely be applied to the study of any eco-narrative. Moreover, as "plasti(e)cological thinking" suggests that this sort of epistemological framework stands grounded in the "lines of flight", it can facilitate one making inroads into any generic work. This is precisely one of the reasons why Roy's eco-narrative, that is, *How I Became a Tree*, in spite of having a non-fictional identity, is considered to lay out the flexibility and viability across genres.

In the opening part titled "A Tree Grew Inside My Head", Roy engages herself in exploring a unique concept like "tree time" which, unlike the human configuration of temporality, stands deeply connected to different planetary "elements". In "Tree Time", Roy strikingly reflects:

> I wanted to become a tree because trees did not wear bras. Then it had to do with the spectre of violence. I loved the way in trees coped with dark and lonely places while sunlessness decided curfew hours for me. I liked too how trees thrived on things that were freely available–water, air and sunlight; and no mortgage in spite of their lifelong occupation of land. (3)

Roy is clear in saying that the act of becoming a tree entails the cessation of the human way of leading a life on the planet Earth. It is by means of cutting oneself off from the spheres of human ecology, the speaker here wishes to take a plunge into the life of a tree. This is possible at least at the level of ecological discourses because of the inherent plasticity of planetary ecology. Trees like other planetary entities are quite dependent on geological resources of the planet and constantly interact with the Earth through "eco-logics"[3]. The speaker feels: "A tree was a daily wage labourer, in its life of work bound to the cycle of sunlight" (3). It means that like human beings, a tree, too, exerts efforts to stand in tune with the "cycle of sunlight" and unlike human beings who are used to getting holidays, ". . . vacations, weekends, the salaried life, pension and loans" (3), a tree seems to be satisfied with some basic minimums from the natural world. It means that the speaker is really tired of hectic human "life" and thus wishes to step into the process of becoming a tree:

> I was tired of speed. I wanted to live to tree time. . . . A tree did not stay up all night to become a successful examinee the next morning. Plant life, in spite of its various genres of seasonal flowers and fruits, did not–could not–do that. One can't tinker with the timing of a yawn, one cannot play with tree time. (4)
>
> I wandered aimlessly through philosophical discussions on time until it came to me one night, in my salty sleep: carpe diem, seize the moment, living in the present–that tree time, a life without worries for the future or regret for the past. (6)

The speaker seems to have explicitly argued that she is dissatisfied with the way her life goes on and wants to emulate "plant life" simply because nobody can toy with "tree time". In other words, a tree has its individuality which has distinctive manifestation that does not necessarily comply with human-centric ideas. Roy's understanding of "tree time" is suggestive of how she inclines to be united with the "present" instead of either delving deeper into the past or figuring out the future. Here, one may critically argue that Roy could think of "becoming" a tree because she seems to be acquainted with the plasticity of ecology. Moreover, plants, as Roy pertinently argues, ate:

> . . . only as much as they needed, and so they suffered neither from obesity nor malnutrition. In plant economics, need and want are one and the same thing, unlike in the human world where wants had the character of a capitalist bulldozer whose actions could be justified through the prettified word 'desire'. (11)

So, it is obvious that plants seem to be more intelligent than human beings who exploit natural resources thereby putting the Earth in jeopardy. Therefore, Roy's "becoming a tree" is implicative of her desire to restore order and balance in life. She understands that interactions between planetary ecologies do not get affected and disrupted as long as the Earth remains unexploited and un-hurt. "Plasti(e)cological thinking" here can be employed to contend that plant life is neither "inferior" nor exclusive to human life; rather it is a part of the "in-tensive totality" totality of planetary ecology that stands mediated through a number of earthly elements. Roy is of this standpoint that ". . . so plants con-tinue to remain ahistorical creatures" (16) thereby suggesting that plants do not comply with the human conceptualization of time and thus can confidently transgress the bounds and territories of temporality. Here, "plasti(e)cological thinking" comes into play in that it helps one understand how plants resort to "lines of flight"[4] and "rhizomatic" growth to cross over the limits of time.

Roy's "becoming a tree" connotes how a tree chooses to grow at its disposal and does not follow any preordained pattern of growth: "To be more precise, it was the geometry of unpredictability–the tree was expected to grow branches at certain intervals, alternating between right and left, and always in a linear fashion, never curving on itself or refusing to grow" (52). It is "the geometry of unpredictability" that drives Roy to take a plunge into the "plant life". "Plasti(e)cological thinking" can be used here to explain how the development of a tree is a matter of "filiation" whereas a "rhizome" stands embedded in the matter of "alliance". Therefore, the "plant life" is at the bottom connected to a number of "matters" including "bio-geo-eco-atmospheres". Yet, Roy is quite aware of the way trees are frequently cut down to serve a number of human luxuries and thus rightfully said:

> Trees do not deserve this. They do not commit crimes. And yet they are given capital punishment.
> Do men kill trees the way they kill fellow humans? What is the difference between the two assignations? Animals might kill plants for food, man is the only animal that kills trees for wood. (218)

Following this excerpt, one may argue that "plant life" is approached by men and animals in different ways and this difference speaks of the exploitative and consumerist attitudes of the human world. Here, "plasti(e)cological thinking" leads one to argue that attempts to territorialize "plant life" for the human world alone trigger ecological violence that ends up in dismantling and dis-rupting symbiotic synthesis existing in the planetary ecology.

Roy's *How I Became a Tree* has to be taken into account as an important eco-narrative, for it does not only relate Roy's personal attachment with the idea of "becoming a tree" but also helps one think through and beyond "plant life" that transversally cuts across flows, folds and circulation of planetary ecology. The embodiment of "plant life" through different forms is steeped in "kinesis" and thus is conditioned by the geological movements of the Earth. It has now become clear that "plasti(e)cological thinking" is one such important epistemological framework that helps one connect the various folds of planetary ecology in general and particularly map ceaseless interactions and intersections among different elements of planetary ecology. Efficacy of "plasti(e)cological thinking" in deciphering the transformative and transformational potentials of planetary ecology is beyond any doubt inasmuch as it stands wedded to "the production of the new" and hence elusive to coding and stratification. As far as the act of becoming is concerned, "plasti(e)cological thinking" can alone help one figure out the way Roy intends to take up the "lines of flight" to step into the world of trees.

Notes

1. In *Infrathin: An Experiment in Micropoetics*, Marjorie Perloff elucidates "micropoetics" in the following words: ". . . [Micropoetics privileges] the context– history, geography, culture–of a given poem's conception and reception are always central" (12).
2. In "Asphyxia", Sen uncovers the appalling impacts of air pollution on the human world and how it gets diffused into the physical ecologies of the world:

> our breath, our words wheezing
> in pulmonary distress. How many masks?
> do you need to mask the bloated AQI scale?
> Callousness breed calluses in our lungs,
> pollutants lacerate our larynx, breathlessness
> wheeze. This deathly gas chamber
> this Capital melancholy, this burning crop,
> this building dust, factor fumes, pestilence–
> *Sweet* Yamuna *run softly till I end my*
> smog–this insidious dirge, this unripe rot. (*Anthropocene* 37)

3. See Ghosh's article "Globing the Earth: The New Eco-logics of Nature" that build up a new "eco-logics" by means of foregrounding fluidity and transgressivity of Nature.
4. See *A Thousand Plateaus* written by Deleuze and Guattari who contend: "It is on lines of flight that new weapons are invented, to be turned against the heavy arms of the State" (204). Therefore, it refers to the forces of deterritorialization that is instrumental in freeing something from the clutches of authority.

Works Cited

Deleuze, Gilles and Felix Guattari. *A Thousand Plateaus: Capitalism and Schizophrenia.* University of Minnesota Press, 1987.

Ghosh, Ranjan. "Globing the Earth: The New Eco-logics of Nature." *SubStance,* vol. 41, no. 1, 2012, pp. 3-14. https://doi.org/10.1353/sub.2012.0008

Herzogenrath, Bernd. "White Ecology." *Prismatic Ecology: Ecotheory beyond Green,* edited by Jeffrey Jerome Cohen, University of Minnesota Press, 2013, pp. 1-21.

Perloff, Marjorie. *Infrathin: An Experiment in Micropoetics.* The University of Chicago Press, 2021.

Roy, Sumana. *How I Became a Tree.* Aleph, 2017.

Sen, Sudeep. *Anthropocene: Climate Change, Contagion, Consolation.* Pippa Rann Books and Media, 2021.

–. *EroText: desire, disease, delusion, dream, downpour.* Penguin, 2019.

Conclusion - "Zoegraphy": Working out an (Infra)structural Geoerotics

This chapter aims at providing a brief mapping of what I have already argued in the previous chapters and in doing so, it seeks to discuss the notion of "zoegraphy" in connection with "plasti(e)cological thinking", thereby making attempts to configure and analyze a "poetics of molecularity"– a food for thought for those who are interested in taking up the loose ends of this book further. Furthermore, it is also intended to work out a "smooth" (infra)structural geoerotics which may provide useful and relevant insights to stretch the epistemic limits of plasti(e)cological thinking. The notion of "zoegraphy" is fast emerging and is intended to be theorized not just only to help critical thinkers moving beyond the peripheries of "bio-centric" approaches to the world around us but also to facilitate them to embrace posthuman ways of knowing the world whose "intensive multiplicity"[1] and "differential relations"[2] are worth exploring with the help of "molecular thinking".

In the Introduction, attempts have been made to analyze why ecopoetical thoughts nowadays cannot help one answer questions on the deplorable conditions of planetary ecology. Certain epistemological questions are deliberately put forward in the beginning to unsettle one's understanding of ecopoetics and its relevance today. This is intended not just only to unsettle critical thinkers' long-standing intellectual engagements with Ecopoetics but also to make them rethink how ecopoetical insights can be updated by means of tinkering with the strands of planetarity. In other words, epistemological limits of ecopoetics are laid bare to argue that if ecopoetics has to work effectively in the contemporary times, it has to be reinvented with the help of deterritorialization–a Deleuzo-Guattarian formulation which is extensively employed to tinker ecopoetics with the tenets of planetarity. Ecopoetical thoughts reflected in Vedic hymns are considered to help readers know the nascent state of ecopoetics. It is then posited in contrast with the advancements of ecopoetics at the turn of the previous century as a critical tool of inquiry. Various dimensions of contemporary ecopoetics are drawn to lay bare how much it has progressed since its ancient figurations. It is by contrasting contemporary viewpoints on ecopoetics against its ancient counterparts, epistemological loopholes of ecopoetics are underscored thereby making the ground ready for tinkering with planetarity. Deterritorialization of ecopoetics entails refashioning of planetarity which lays down the ground for the theorization of "plasti(e)cological thinking".

In Chapter I, the concept of planetarity is explored from a number of critical standpoints thereby intending to bring out the multifacetedness of planetarity. Initially, reflections of planetary thinking in Vedic hymns are mapped to underscore how Vedic sages used to engage themselves with "planetarity". It is shapely pitted against contemporary planetary thinking so as to help readers understand how the notion of planetarity has acquired several dimensions over time. It leads me to arrive at that over a period of time, the notion of planetarity has got caught up in the process of stratification and thus needs a systematic ungrounding. Therefore, destratifying "planetarity" is planned to upgrade with the help of Deleuze and Guattari. It is followed by a close investigation of "planetary illness" and how it stands vulnerable to global capitalism. The notion of "New Earth" is taken into account to argue that the purview of planetary thinking needs to be broadened to examine how global capitalism and its vicious variants including neoliberalism strikes at the wellbeing of the planet so that the notion of planetarity could be held as an "integrative project" instead of being called as a stratified material/discursive design.

In Chapter II, the concept of "plasti(e)cological thinking" is critically configured and subsequently put forward. Distinctive configuration of "plasti(e)cological thinking" is analyzed by taking recourse to a number of critical thinkers. Salient strands of "plasti(e)cological thinking" are subtly weaved together with the tenets of posthumanist ideas, thereby making the former conceptually stronger. Connections between "plasti(e)cological thinking" and "posthuman turns" conditioned by the pervasive trajectories of planetarity are established to show the viability and applicability of "plasti(e)cological thinking" in contemporary times. "Plasti(e)cological thinking" is configured in such a way that it can help one transgress so-called stratified ecologies on the Earth. Fluid intersectionality existing among various planetary ecologies can best be investigated by "plasti(e)cological thinking" which facilitates one to go beyond segmented and territorialized understanding of planetarity.

In Chapter III, three Indian eco-texts are drawn to validate how "plasti(e)cological thinking" in reality helps one traverse the flows, folds and circulations of planetary ecology. Apart from showing the efficacy of "plasti(e)cological thinking" with particular references to select Indian eco-texts, this chapter seeks to bring out why it is important to go beyond the limits of stratified planetarity by means of working out "plasti(e)cological thinking" as an advanced way of knowing the mediatedness of planetary ecology.

At this point, one may stop and think: how far is it possible for "plasti(e)co-logical thinking" to interrogate the limits of stratified planetarity? Is it possible to develop "plasti(e)cological thinking" further? Where to does "plasti(e)colog-ical thinking" lead us? Answers to these questions are planned to be found out in the subsequent paragraphs so as to open up new possibilities embedded in the critical construct called "plasti(e)cological thinking". It has now become clear that "plasti(e)cological thinking" is quite capable of traversing diverse folds of planetary ecology seamlessly and this is possible because of the fact that the configuration of "plasti(e)cological thinking" stands distant from an-thropocentric dialecticism between "bio" and "eco", and embedded in the traversal trajectories of "zoe", an abstraction of "life". Whereas "bio" refers to physical figurations of "life" in reality, "zoe" is elusive, slippery, deterritorial, transgressive, fluid, "trans(in)fusive" and transcorporeal in nature. In "Zoegra-phy: Per/forming Posthuman Lives", Louis Van Den Hengel works out the notion of "zoegraphy" in the following terms:

> I want to call this approach *zoegraphy*, a mode of writing life that is not indexed on the traditional notion of *bios*–the discursive, social, and po-litical life appropriate to human beings–but which centers on the generative vitality of *zoe*, an inhuman, impersonal, and inorganic force which . . . is not specific to human lifeworlds, but cuts across humans, animals, technologies, and things. *Zoegraphy* is my attempt to confront the question of how to think and how to write a life that does not have any human body or self at its center, a life which is in fact fundamentally inhuman, yet which connects human life to the immanent forces of a vital materiality. (2)

Hengel makes a couple of points very clear here: the first being the existing dif-ference between "bios" and "zoe" and the second being the formulation of a critical approach called "zoegraphy" to examine the nuanced connections be-tween human "life" and "the immanent forces of a vital materiality" that is, the non-human world. Following Hengel's theoretical construction, it is con-tended that the constitutive strands of "plasti(e)cological thinking" stand enmeshed with the tenets of "zoegraphy" in many ways. For example, whereas "zoegraphy" speaks of a departure from the corporeal incarceration of "life" within rigid and inflexible bodies to a more supple, plastic and fluid figuration of "life" that is wedded to the "immanent forces of a vital materiality", "plasti(e)cological thinking" in actuality pertains to this operative logic of "zo-egraphy". It means that "plasti(e)cological thinking" seeks to investigate how the vibrancy of each "fold", "flow" and "circulation" of planetary ecology stands conditioned by the "nomadic singularities" or "differential intensities". Inhuman and inorganic forms of "life" embodied by "zoe" is the operative factor by means of which "smooth politics"[3] engages human and non-human worlds in a series of transcorporeal and trans(in)fusive interactions across the "Plane of Consistency".

Configuration of "zoe" has further been worked out by Rosi Braidotti in *The Posthuman* where she cogently reflects:

> I, therefore, do not work completely within the social constructivist method but rather emphasize the non-human, vital force of Life, which is what I have coded as *zoe*. . . . *Zoe* as the dynamic, self-organizing structure of life itself (Braidotti 2006, 2011b) stands for generative vitality. It is the transversal force that cuts across and reconnects previously segregated species, categories and domains. *Zoe-centred* egalitarianism is, for me, the core of the post-anthropocentric turn: it is a materialist, secular, grounded and unsentimental response to the opportunistic transspecies commodification of Life that is the logic of advanced capitalism. (60)

Braidotti goes a step further here and contends that "zoe" happens to be a "generative vitality" that plays an instrumental role in dismantling and disrupting patterns of global capitalism spread across the world. Interestingly, unlike "bio", "zoe" is a "dynamic" force which is capable of cutting across and reconnecting "segregated species, categories and domains" thereby suggesting how "zoe" performs a veritable conduit between distant ecologies. Braidotti also clarifies that "zoe" is able to cater a "materialist, secular, grounded and unsentimental response" to the oppressive and repressive mechanisms of global capitalism. This operative dimension of "zoe" can tenably be taken into account to schizophrenize "plasti(e)cological thinking" further inasmuch as "zoegraphical" insights are steeped in what Thomas Nail calls "kinopolitics"[4] and Deleuze and Guattari call "supple segmentarity". In short, as "plasti(e)cological thinking" is linked up "with the productive and immanent force of zoe, or life in its non-human aspects" (Braidotti 66), it can effectively dismiss the processes of hierarchization, territorialization and stratification backed up by the pervasive agencies of global capitalism.

Differential processuality of "zoe" can hardly be overlooked, for it is responsible for the intensive becomings of planetary ecology. Braidotti particularly underlines transversal dimensions of "zoe" while working out its affect(abilities):

Transversality actualizes zoe-centred egalitarianism as an ethics and also
as a method to account for forms of alternative, posthuman subjectivity.
An ethics based on the primacy of the relation, of interdependence, values *zoe* in itself. (95)
A nomadic zoe-centred approach connects human to non-human life
so as to develop a comprehensive eco-philosophy of becoming. (104)

Following Braidotti's standpoint, this can be argued that "zoegraphical" interventions seem to be helpful in expanding the horizon of "plasti(e)cological
thinking" in that it can facilitate one to think through and beyond the notion of
plasti(e)cology so as to work out an "eco-philosophy of becoming". In a nutshell, "*zoe*-political" dimensions of planetarity need to be explored with the
help of "plasti(e)cological thinking" so that hitherto unexplored dimensions of
planetarity can be brought out. Therefore, epistemic integration of
"plasti(e)cological thinking" with "zoegraphy" leads one to arrive at that ". . .
we inhabit in a world that is neither anthropocentric nor anthropomorphic, but
rather geo-political, ecosophical and proudly *zoe*-centered" (Braidotti 194).

Here, one may also be induced to bring in what Deleuze and Guattari
call "molecular" thinking to explore the nuances of "*zoe*-politics". In
other words, schizophrenic interventions into the ontological fluidity of
"*zoe*-politics" can be deciphered with the help of "molecular" thinking.
In *Anti-Oedipus*, Deleuze and Guattari ingeniously reflect:
Schizophrenia or desiring-production is the boundary between the molar organization and the molecular multiplicity of desire; this limit of
deterritorialization must now pass into the interior of the molar organization, and it must be applied to a factitious and subjugated territoriality.
(102)

It suggests that molecular thinking is premised on "infinitesimal lines of escape" (*Anti-Oedipus*; 280), which is required for making epistemic inroads into
the fluid configuration of "*zoe*-politics". Molecular intensities of "*zoe*-politics"
need to be mapped to figure out how "plasti(e)cological thinking" can be tuned
in line with molecular thinking. What is interesting is that molecular thinking
seems to be capable of explaining to all that molecular configuration lies enfolded within molar counterpart and molecular alterations at the intensive
level result in the refashioning of molar aggregates. In the case of planetary
ecology, molecular thinking may lead one to make full use of "*zoe*-politics" to
stretch the epistemic limits of "plasti(e)cological thinking" further.

In *A Thousand Plateaus*, Deleuze and Guattari have further elaborated molecular thinking by means of grounding the logic of micropolitics. It is argued here that "molecular multiplicities" or "molecular assemblage of enunciation" (84) can be figured out by means of making a micropolitical engagement with the notion of molecularity. Deleuze and Guattari have commented on the overlapping between molecular lines and micropolitics in the following words:

> This molecular line, more supple but no less disquieting, in fact, much more disquieting, is not simply internal or personal: it also brings everything into play, but on a different scale and in different forms, with segmentations of a different nature, rhizomatic instead of arborescent. A micropolitics. (199)

It is clear that micropolitics could be taken into consideration as a useful critical tool to figure out "molecular lines" that stand embedded in "*zoe*-politics". Micropolitics allows one to pursue pre-physical singularities of "zoe" which contributes to the making of molecularity. Although it is true that in every politics, micropolitics remains folded into macropolitics, there exists ". . . a micropolitics of perception, affection, conversation, and so forth" (1987 213). One has to try to figure out "micropercepts" to get to the bottom of "a micropolitics of perception and affection". In other words, affective potentials of micropolitics could be used to step into the poetics of molecularity[5] that is instrumental in knowing and doing "*zoe*-politics"–a "zoegraphical" intervention which can facilitate one to explore "plasti(e)cological thinking" further, overstepping the epistemic constraints of stratified planetarity.

In addition to it, the epistemic configuration of "smooth" (infra)structural geoerotics needs to be unpacked to lay out how "plasti(e)cological thinking" facilitates one to transgress the territories of stratified planetarity. Put in simple words, a "smooth" (infra)structural geoerotics stands grounded in the nuanced intersections among deterritorial becomings, (infra)-affective politics and geoerotical assemblage. In *A Thousand Plateaus*, Deleuze and Guattari cogently remark:

> The diagrammatic or abstract machine does not function to represent, even something real, but rather constructs a real that is yet to come, a new type of reality. (1987 142)
> Sometimes one goes from chaos to the threshold of a territorial assemblage: directional components, infra-assemblage. Sometimes one organizes the assemblage: dimensional components, intra-assemblage. (1987 312)

While spelling out the nuanced function of an "abstract machine", Deleuze and Guattari reflect that the operative logic of an "abstract machine" is contingent upon "diagrammatic" progression characterized by "lines of flight" or the forces of deterritorialization and thus is capable of evading back pull off "a territorial assemblage" or a "refrain". Interestingly, the deterritorial trajectory of an "abstract machine" points at the "new" emergent reality, which serves to "pilot" the ceaseless departure of reality from the very process of being in the "refrain". What is even more interesting is that a "diagrammatic" machine "refrains" itself from offering rigid infrastructure, for it seeks to "connect" one assemblage to another assemblage on the "Plane of Consistency" thereby suggesting the "smooth" overlapping between "directional" and "dimensional" strands of an assemblage. Besides it, one may argue that a "diagrammatic" machinic thinking embodied by "plasti(e)cological thinking" pertains to What Deleuze and Guattari call a "short-term memory" which is ". . . in no way subject to a law of contiguity . . . and is always under conditions of discontinuity, rupture, and multiplicity" (1987, 16). It means that just like a rhizomatic becoming of a "short-term memory", "plasti(e)cological thinking" helps one sidestep *contiguity-continuity* dynamics laid down by territorial assemblages and usher in "a new type of reality" by means of effectualizing *discontiguity-discontinuity* matrix which can only offer "smooth" (infra)structural geoerotical insights.

Besides it, (infra)-affective politics can be understood as a decalcomaniac affectivity which can politically be regulated to channel "smooth" flows of (infra)structural geoerotical thoughts. (Infra)-affective politics stands in conformity with what Helene Frichot hails as "infrastructural affects" and with Samuel Weber's "aporetical" conceptualization of 'singularity'.

> Infrastructural affects concern those affects that run through infrastructural systems. Less than attempting to predetermine affect by way of a series of design moves, the emphasis here is rather on fostering spaces of support where affect manifests as a powerful means of getting along together. (Frichot 15)
> The singular must necessarily take leave of what it might have been in order to become what it (never) was; but what it then becomes is no longer purely singular but merely signifies a certain tension between what it might have been and what it could not be. (Weber 18)

Following these two critical observations, it can be argued that (infra)-affective politics actually effectuates "infrastructural affects" by means of being "differentiated"[6] by the strands of "aporetical" singularity. In other words, (infra)-

affective politics allows affective flows of (infra)structure which end up exem-
plifying "aporetical" singularity which ". . . is a repetition that is composed not
just of similarity, but of irreducible difference" (Weber 2). (Infra)-affective politics, thus, seems to be capable of accounting for the "diagrammatic"
cartography that an (infra)structure "pilots" while following "singular" lines of
rupture. The working of (infra)-affective politics actually follow Deleuzean understanding of "singularity" in *The Logic of Sense*:

> . . . singularities possess a process of auto-unification, always mobile
> and displaced to the extent that a paradoxical element traverses the se-
> ries and makes them resonate, enveloping the corresponding singular
> points in a single aleatory point . . . in a single cast. (103)

It suggests that the domain of "plasti(e)cological thinking" can epistemologi-
cally be stretched off to the extent that it can help one figure out the nuanced
correspondences between 'singular' points on an aleatory point of departure
so as to "refrain" "plasti(e)cological thinking" from getting territorialized. (Infra)-affective politics lays down "singular" and "diagrammatic" "lines of
becoming" that empower "plasti(e)cological thinking" to take off from the
points of "connective synthesis" so as to actualize what Arjen Kleinherenbrink
calls in *Against Continuity* "disjunctive synthesis"[7] of aleatory points, thereby
making room for geoerotical assemblages to come into actions.

The notion of geoerotics stands linked up to the complex deterritorial progression of desire which at once seeks to function as an (infra)-affective liaison
between the forces of territorialization and deterritorialization, and at times
serves to work as a "circuit-breaker" to the logic of capitalistic productivity. Geoerotics refers to the differential process by means of which the Earth stands in
transit and gets transformed and trans(in)fused. As "plasti(e)cological thinking" seeks to strike a departure from the limit of stratified planetarity, it has to
be positioned within the chaosophical immanentism of the Earth which func-
tions as a "body without organs" (BwO):

> The object of desire must in fact restrict itself to being nothing more
> than this response; that is, it must no longer exist for itself but for the
> other's desire. (Bataille 143)
> Desire is never separable from complex assemblages that necessarily tie
> into molecular levels, from microforma-tions already shaping postures,
> attitudes, perceptions, expectations, semiotic systems, etc. Desire is
> never an undifferentiated instinctual energy, but itself results from a

highly developed, engineered setup rich in interactions: a whole supple segmentarity. . . . (Deleuze and Guattari, 1987 215)

Following these two critical observations, one may critically reflect that the formation of the function of a geoerotical assemblage is regulated by (infra)structural affects and deterritorial becomings. It means that a geoerotical assemblage offers a fluid lay-out which facilitates "(infra)structural affects" to step in the lines of "supple segmentarity" thereby producing aleatory points of departure which are of profound import to destratify "plasti(e)ecological thinking". As "plasti(e)ecological thinking" carries the "earth" within it, it cannot help being governed by geoerotical assemblages which, being grouped together with deterritorial becomings, (infra)-affective politics and (infra)structural affects, seem to be capable of calling sedentary and stratified, overcoded and territorial workings of planetarity into question. In fact, one can think of working out bio/eco-semiotics to advance "plasti(e)ecological thinking" further. In an interesting article "From Thing to Relation. On Bateson's Bioanthropology" Jesper Hoffmeyer cogently puts forward: "Pleroma like firstness can only be cogitized through its appearences in our cognitive system, so pleroma might perhaps be said to correspond to firstness in its being in itself. . ." (31). Hoffmeyer clearly articulates how "pleroma" gets "cogitized" in our cognitive system and how it finely corresponds to the "firstness" of an idea much before its materialization. Following Hoffmeyer's insight, one may critically reflect that "plasti(e)ecological thinking" could actually lay out "pleromatic phenomenon" (31) while exploiting "smooth" (infra)structural geoerotics so as to underpin nuanced and seamless synthesis between human and non-human worlds. In short, "plasti(e)ecological thinking" stands capable of "piloting" the production of the "new" in the "zones of irreducibilities" and thus can potentially encourage critical thinkers to get engaged in exploring bio/eco-semiotical possibilities for the sake of nuanced understanding of the emergent New Earth.

Notes

1. In *A Thousand Plateaus*, Deleuze and Guattari reflect:
    . . . intensive multiplicities composed of particles that do not divide without changing in nature, and distances that do not vary without entering another multiplicity and that constantly construct and dismantle themselves in the course of their communications, as they cross over into each other at, beyond, or before a certain threshold. (33)
2. In *Difference and Repetition*, Deleuze expatiates on the idea of differential relation and how it stands connected to the interplay between "differen*t*iation" and "differen*c*iation":

We call the determination of the virtual content of an Idea differen*t*iation; we call the actualisation of that virtuality into species and distinguished parts differen-*c*iation. It is always in relation to a differen*t*iated problem or to the differen*t*iated conditions of a problem that a differen*c*iation of species and parts is carried out. ... (207)

3. See Malcolm Bull's article titled "Smooth Politics" which refers to the distinctive fea-tures of it "smooth politics" in contrast with "striated" politics: "Whereas traditional politics presupposes the social, in a smooth world you can have a politics without a soci-ology, a politics of unimpeded movement" (226).

4. In "Kinopolitics: Borders in Motion", Thomas Nail hails 'kinopolitics' as "the theory and analysis of social motion" (190). In short, Nail thinks that "kinopolitics" ". . . is pre-cisely the analysis of social flows" (191). Three basic pillars of "kinopolitics" include "flow", "fold" and "circulation".

5. In "Molar and molecular mobilities: The politics of perceptible and imperceptible movements", Peter Merriman cogently argues: "Molecular movements generate tension and emerge where two or more bodies are attuned and possess the capacity to affect or be affected" (14). Merriman means to say that "the poetics of molecularity" stands di-vested of binaries, dualities and dialecticism.

6. In *Difference and Repetition*, Deleuze argues: "Whereas differentiation determines the virtual content of the Idea as a problem, differenciation expresses the actualisation of this virtual and the constitution of solutions (by local integrations)" (209).

7. In *Against Continuity*, Arjen Kleinherenbrink cogently reflects that "disjunctive syn-thesis" tells ". . . us that a relation is not just the contraction of other machines into actuality, but that this happens because of an activation of the powers of a machine" (189). It means that "disjunctive synthesis" accounts for the actualization of a machinic assemblage which operates on the "Plane of Consistency" and forges "zones of irreduci-bility" that works as an impetus for the production of the "new" to which "plasti(e)cological thinking" stands wedded to.

Works Cited

Bataille, Georges. *The Accursed Share: An Essay on General Economy*. Translated by Robert Hurley, Zone Books, 1991.

Braidotti, Rosi. *The Posthuman*. Polity Press, 2013.

Bull, Malcolm. "Smooth Politics." *Empire's New Clothes Reading Hardt and Negri*, edited by Paul A. Passavant and Jodi Dean, Routledge, 2004, pp. 220-233.

Deleuze, Gilles. *Difference and Repetition*. Translated by Paul Patton, Columbia University Press, 1994.

–. and Felix Guattari. *A Thousand Plateaus: Capitalism and Schizophrenia*. Translated by Brian Massumi, University of Minnesota Press, 1987.

–. *Anti-Oedipus: Capitalism and Schizophrenia*. Translated by Robert Hurley, Mark Seem, and Helen R. Lane. University of Minnesota Press, 1983.

–. *The Logic of Sense*. Translated by Mark Lester, The Athlone Press, 1990.

Frichot, Helene. "Infrastructural affects: Challenging the autonomy of architecture." *Architectural Affects after Deleuze and Guattari*, edited by Marko Jobst and Hélène Frichot, Routledge, 2021, pp. 10-25.

Hengel, Louis Van Den. "Zoegraphy: Per/forming Posthuman Lives." *Biography*, vol. 35, no. 1, 2012, pp. 1-20. https://doi.org/10.1353/bio.2012.0003.

Hoffmeyer, Jesper. "From Thing to Relation. On Bateson's Bioanthropology." *A Legacy for Living Systems: Gregory Bateson as Precursor to Biosemiotics*, edited by Hoffmeyer, Springer, 2008, pp. 27-44.

Kleinherenbrink, Arjen. *Against Continuity: Gilles Deleuze's Speculative Realism*. Edinburgh University Press, 2019.

Merriman, Peter. "Molar and molecular mobilities: The politics of perceptible and imperceptible movements." *Environment and Planning D: Society and Space*, vol. 37, no. 1, 2019, pp. 65-82. https://doi.org/10.1177%2F026377 5818776976.

Nail, Thomas. "Kinopolitics: Borders in Motion." *Posthuman Ecologies Complexity and Process after Deleuze*, edited by Rosi Braidotti and Simone Bignall, Rowman and Littlefield, 2019, pp. 183-204.

Weber, Samuel. *Singularity: Politics and Poetics*. University of Minnesota Press, 2021.

Select Bibliography

Alaimo, Stacy. "Violate-Black." *Prismatic Ecology: Ecotheory beyond Green*, edited by Jeffrey Jerome Cohen, 2013, pp. 233-251.

Barthes, Roland. *Mythologies*. The Noonday Press, 1957.

Bataille, Georges. *The Accursed Share: An Essay on General Economy*. Translated by Robert Hurley, Zone Books, 1991.

Bhandar, Brenna, and Jonathan Goldberg-Hiller. "Introduction: Staging Encounters." In *Plastic Materialities: Politics, Legality and Metamorphosis in the Work of Catherine* Malabou, edited by Bhandar and Goldberg-Hiller, Duke Up, 2015, pp. 1-33.

Bignall, Simone, and Rosi Braidotti. "Posthuman Systems." *Posthuman Ecologies Complexity and Process after Deleuze*, edited by Braidotti and Bignall, Rowman and Littlefield, 2019, pp. 1-16.

Bogue, Ronald. "A Thousand Ecologies." In *Deleuze/Guattari & Ecology*, edited by Bernd Herzogenrath, Palgrave Macmillan, 2009, pp. 42-56.

Braidotti, Rosi. *The Posthuman*. Polity Press, 2013.

Brydson, J. A. *Plastic Materials*. Butterworth-Heinemann, 1999.

Bryson, J. Scott. "Preface." *The West Side of Any Mountain: Place, Space, and Ecopoetry*, by Bryson, University of Iowa Press, 2005, pp. 1-6.

Bull, Malcolm. "Smooth Politics." Empire's New Clothes Reading Hardt and Negri, edited by Paul A. Passavant and Jodi Dean, Routledge, pp. 220-233.

Campos, Isabel Sobral. "Introduction Transnational Ecopoetics." *Ecopoetics and the Global Landscape: Critical Essays*, edited by Campos, Lexington Books, 2019, pp. ix-xvii.

Chakraborty, Dipesh. "The Planet: An Emergent Humanist Category." *Critical Inquiry*, vol. 46, 2019, pp. 1-31. 00093-1896/19/4601-0002.

–. *The Climate of History in a Planetary Age*. The University of Chicago Press, 2021.

Cohen, Tom. "The Angel and the Storm "Material Spirit" in the Era of Climate Change." *Material Spirit Religion and Literature Intranscendent*, edited by Gregory C. Stallings, Manuel Asensi, and Carl Good, Fordham University Press, 2014, pp. 129-153.

Conley, Verena Andermatt. *Ecopolitics: The environment in poststructuralist thought*. Routledge, 2006.

Deleuze, Gilles. *Difference and Repetition*. Translated by Paul Patton, Columbia University Press, 1994.

–. *The Logic of Sense*. Translated by Mark Lester, The Athlone Press, 1990.

–, and Felix Guattari. *A Thousand Plateaus: Capitalism and Schizophrenia*. Translated by Brian Massumi, University of Minnesota Press, 1987.

–. *Anti-Oedipus: Capitalism and Schizophrenia.* Translated by Robert Hurley, Mark Seem, and Helen R. Lane. University of Minnesota Press, 1983.

–. *What is Philosophy?* Columbia University Press, 1994.

Derrida, Jacques. *The Animal That Therefore I Am.* Edited by Marie-Luise Mallet, Fordham University Press, 2008.

Elias, Amy J., and Christian Moraru. "Introduction: The Planetary Condition." *The Planetary Turn Relationality and Geoaesthetics in the Twenty-First Century*, edited by Elias and Moraru, Northwestern University Press, 2015, pp. xi-xxxvii.

Evans, Brad, and Julian Reid. *Resilient Life: The Art of Living Dangerously.* Polity Press, 2014.

Evernden, Neil. "Beyond Ecology: SELF, PLACE, AND THE PATHETIC FALLACY." *The Ecocriticism Reader: Landmark in Literary Ecology*, edited by Glotfelty and Harold Fromm, The University of Georgia Press, 1996, pp. 102-103.

Frichot, Helene. "Infrastructural affects: Challenging the autonomy of architecture." *Architectural Affects after Deleuze and Guattari*, edited by Marko Jobst and Hélène Frichot, Routledge, 2021, pp. 10-25.

Garrard, Greg. *Ecocriticism.* Routledge, 2004.

Ghosh, Ranjan. "Globing the Earth: The New Eco-logics of Nature." *SubStance*, vol. 41, no. 1, 2012, pp. 3-14. https://doi.org/10.1353/sub.2012.0008.

Ghosh, Ranjan. "Plastic Literature." *University of Toronto Quarterly*, vol. 88, no. 2, 2019, pp. 277-291. https://muse.jhu.edu/article/732562.

–. "The Plastic Controversy." *Critical Inquiry*, Feb. 4, 2021. https://critinq.wordpress.com/2021/02/04/the-plastic-controversy/.

–. *Trans(in)fusion: Reflections for Critical Thinking.* Routledge, 2021.

Glotfelty, Cheryll. Introduction: Literary Studies in an Age of Environmental Crisis. *The Ecocriticism Reader: Landmark in Literary Ecology*, edited by Glotfelty and Harold Fromm, The University of Georgia Press, 1996, pp. xv-xxxvii.

Griffith, Ralph T. H, translator. *The Hymns of the Atharvaveda.* Global Grey Ebooks, 1896.

–. translator. *The Hymns of the R̥gveda.* Motilal Banarsidass, 1896.

Guattari, Felix. *The Three Ecologies.* Translated by Ian Pindar and Paul Sutton, The Athlone Press, 2000.

–. *Schizoanalytic Cartographies.* Translated by Andrew Goffey, Bloomsbury, 2013.

Harvey, David. *A Brief History of Neoliberalism.* Oxford University Press, 2005.

Hengel, Louis Van Den. "Zoegraphy: Per/forming Posthuman Lives." *Biography*, vol. 35, no. 1, 2012, pp. 1-20. https://doi.org/10.1353/bio.2012.0003.

Herzogenrath, Bernd. "White Ecology." *Prismatic Ecology: Ecotheory beyond Green*, edited by Jeffrey Jerome Cohen, University of Minnesota Press, 2013, pp. 1-21.

Hoffmeyer, Jesper. "From Thing to Relation. On Bateson's Bioanthropology." A Legacy for Living Systems: Gregory Bateson as Precursor to Biosemiotics, edited by Hoffmeyer, Springer, 2008, pp. 27-44.

Ingersoll, Andrew P. *Planetary Climates*. Princeton University Press, 2013.

Judy, Ronald A. T. "Provisional Note on Formations of Planetary Violence." *Boundary* 2 vol. 33, no. 3, 2006, pp. 141-150. DOI 10.1215/01903659-2006-019.

Jue, Melody, and Rafico Ruiz, editors. *Saturation: An Elemental Politics*. Duke UP, 2021.

Kahn, Richard. *Critical Pedagogy, Ecoliteracy, & Planetary Crisis THE ECOPEDA-GOGY MOVEMENT*. Peter Lang, 2010.

Kleinherenbrink, Arjen. *Against Continuity: Gilles Deleuze's Speculative Realism*. Edinburgh University Press, 2019.

Knickerbocker, Scott. "Introduction: The Language of Nature, the Nature of Language." *Ecopoetics: The Language of Nature, the Nature of Language*, by Knickerbocker, University of Massachusetts Press, 2012, pp. 1-18.

Laberge, Jean-Sebastien. "Heterogenesis, Ecosophy and Dissent." *Schizoanalysis and Ecosophy: Reading Deleuze and Guattari*, edited by Constantin V. Boundas, Bloomsbury Academic, 2018, pp. 109-127.

Lattig, Sharon. "Introduction: The Region of the Song." *Cognitive Ecopoetics A New Theory of Lyric*, by Lattig, Bloomsbury Academic, 2021, pp.1-32.

Lemonick, Michael D. "Before the Big Bang." *Discover*, Feb 5, 2004. https://www.discovermagazine.com/the-sciences/before-the-big-bang

Magrane, Eric, et al. *Geopoetics in Practice*. Routledge, 2020.

Malabou, Catherine. *Ontology of the Accident: An Essay on Destructive Plasticity*. Translated by Carolyn Shread, Polity Press, 2012.

–. *The Future of Hegel: Plasticity, Temporality and Dialectic*. Translated by Lisabeth During, Routledge, 2005.

Mentz, Steve. "Brown." *Prismatic Ecology: Ecotheory beyond Green*, edited by Jeffrey Jerome Cohen, 2013, pp. 193-212.

Merriman, Peter. "Molar and molecular mobilities: The politics of perceptible and imperceptible movements." *Environment and Planning D: Society and Space*, vol. 37, no. 1, 2019, pp. 65-82. https://doi.org/10.1177%2F0263775818776976.

Merriam-Webster. *Springfield*, 1831.

Mickey, Sam. *Whole Earth Thinking and Planetary Coexistence: Ecological wisdom at the intersection of religion, ecology, and philosophy*. Routledge, 2016.

Millennium Ecosystem Assessment (MEA). 2005. https://www.millenniumassessment.org/en/index.html. Accessed on Nov. 20, 2021.

Morrison, Susan Signe. *The Literature of Waste Material Ecopoetics and Ethical Matter*. Palgrave Macmillan, 2015.

Morton, Timothy. *Being Ecological*. MIT Press, 2018.

–. *Ecology Without Nature: Rethinking Environmental Aesthetics*. Harvard University Press, 2007.

–. "Coexistence and Coexistents: Ecology without a World." Ecocritical Theory: New European Approaches, edited by Axel Goodbody and Kate Rigby, University of Virginia Press, 2011, pp. 168-180.

Murasawa, Mahoro, and Stéphane Nadaud. "Ecosophy as an ethical mode of existence." *Why Guattari? A Liberation of Cartographies, Ecologies and Politics*, edited by Thomas Jellis, Joe Gerlach, and J. D. Dewsbury, Routledge, 2019, pp. 119-132.

Muzio, Tim Di. *Carbon Capitalism: Energy, Social Reproduction and World Order.* Rowman and Littlefield International Ltd., 2015.

Nail, Thomas. *Theory of the Earth.* Stanford University Press, 2021.

–. "Kinopolitics: Borders in Motion." *Posthuman Ecologies Complexity and Process after Deleuze*, edited by Rosi Braidotti and Simone Bignall, Rowman and Littlefield, 2019, pp. 183-204.

Nicholson, Simon, and Sikina Jinnah. Introduction: Living on a New Earth. *New Earth Politics Essays from the Anthropocene*, edited by, Nicholson and Jinnah, The MIT Press, 2016, pp. 1-16.

Nolan, Sarah. "Un-natural Ecopoetics Natural/Cultural Intersections in Poetic Language and Form." *New International Voices in Ecocriticism*, edited by Serpil Oppermann, Lexington Books, 2015, pp. 87-99.

Oppermann, Serpil. "Introduction New International Voices in Ecocriticism." *New International Voices in Ecocriticism*, edited by Oppermann, Lexington Books, 2015, pp. 1-24.

Parry, Jason. "Philosophy as Terraforming: Deleuze and Guattari on Designing a New Earth." *Diacritics*, vol. 47, no. 3, 2019, pp. 108-138. https://doi.org/10.1353/dia.2019.0028.

Perloff, Marjorie. *Infrathin: An Experiment in Micropoetics.* The University of Chicago Press, 2021.

Philips, Dana. "Is Nature Necessary?" *The Ecocriticism Reader: Landmark in Literary Ecology*, edited by Glotfelty and Harold Fromm, The University of Georgia Press, 1996, pp. 204-224.

Plamondon, Chantal, and Jay Sinha. *Life Without Plastic: The Practical Step-by-Step Guide to Avoiding Plastic to Keep Your Family and the Planet Healthy.* Page Street Publishing, 2017.

Rajan, Chandra, translator. *Kālidāsa: The Loom of Time.* Penguin Books, 1999.

Remmert, Hermann. *Ecology: A Textbook.* Springer-Verlag, 1980.

Rigby, Kate. "Ecopoetics." *Keywords for Environmental Studies*, edited by Joni Adamson, William A. Gleason, and David N. Pellow, New York University Press, 2016, pp. 79-81.

Roy, Sumana. *How I Became a Tree.* Aleph, 2017.

Rueckert, William. "Literature and Ecology: An Experiment in Ecocriticism." *The Ecocriticism Reader: Landmark in Literary Ecology*, edited by Glotfelty and Harold Fromm, The University of Georgia Press, 1996, pp. 105-123.

Saldanha, Arun, and Hannah Stark. "A New Earth: Deleuze and Guattari in the Anthropocene."

Sanders, Scott Russell. "Speaking a Word for Nature." *The Ecocriticism Reader: Landmark in Literary Ecology*, edited by Glotfelty and Harold Fromm, The University of Georgia Press, 1996, pp. 182-195. *Deleuze Studies*, vol. 10, no. 4, 2016, pp. 427-439.

Sauvagnargues, Anne. *ARTMACHINES: Deleuze, Guattari, Simondon*. Edinburgh University Press, 2016.

Sen, Sudeep. *Anthropocene: Climate Change, Contagion, Consolation*. Pippa Rann Books and Media, 2021.

–. *EroText: desire, disease, delusion, dream, downpour*. Penguin, 2019.

Solnick, Sam. *Poetry and the Anthropocene Ecology, biology and technology in contemporary British and Irish poetry*. Routledge, 2017.

Soper, Kate. "Representing Nature." NATURE PROSPECTS, vol. 9, no. 4, 1998, pp. 61-65. https://doi.org/10.1080/10455759809358833

Spivak, Gayatri Chakravorty. *Death of a Discipline*. Columbia University Press, 2003.

Weber, Samuel. *Singularity: Politics and Poetics*. University of Minnesota Press, 2021.

Woodard, Ben. *On an Ungrounded Earth: Towards a New Geophilosophy*. Punctum books, 2013.

Žižek, Slavoj. *Living in the End Times*. Verso, 2011.

Index